"There are very few resources to help childhood trauma survivors effectively navigate the minefield of adult love relationships. Dr. Heather MacIntosh has been a trauma therapist, researcher, and teacher for decades, but in *Healing Broken Bonds*, she also feels like a friend. A survivor herself, she joins her readers on their treacherous path towards earned security with their partners. Her voice is a healing balm for the ravages of early life abuse—an antidote to the overwhelming shame, triggers, and resulting relational patterns that lead survivors to feel isolated and despairing. The workbook makes sense of the impacts of past hurts on present relationships. It is full of helpful explanations, reflection questions, essential tools, and a map to follow towards more safety and connection in adult love."

Alison Carpenter, *Couple Counsellor and Psychotherapist*

"In her latest contribution, Dr. MacIntosh has accomplished something extraordinary in the treatment of couples who are healing from complex trauma. Sharing her deep knowledge and understanding of how human relationships are central to our health, this workbook gives couples a bright, clear light on the path to forging strong, enduring, loving connections. Based on her groundbreaking DCTCT model, this is a workbook that is fully accessible and eminently practical. Recognizing the particular complexities that trauma survivors face in intimate relationships, MacIntosh neither oversimplifies nor overcomplicates the challenges. This workbook, a remarkable integration of all that Dr. MacIntosh has learned from her studies, and most importantly, from her many years of work with couples, will serve as a powerful tool for the many, many couples who are committed to healing and growing together."

Daniel Shaw, *Author*, Traumatic Narcissism: Relational Systems of Subjugation *and*
Traumatic Narcissism and Recovery: Leaving the Prison of Shame and Fear

"This trauma-informed Workbook fills a key gap in the resources available both for trauma survivors as individuals and moreover for couples whose members have been affected by complex trauma. The Workbook provides couples with a highly accessible and exceptionally thorough and well grounded guide for deeply reflecting on and understanding how trauma may be impacting their relationship, and a very practical and engaging introduction to skills for emotion regulation, mentalization, earned security, conjoint memory processing ('telling the story'), and conflict resolution that couples from all walks of life and backgrounds will find exceptionally helpful."

Julian D. Ford, *Ph.D., A.B.P.P., Professor of Psychiatry and Law,*
University of Connecticut Health Center MC1410

"In collaboration with her students and colleagues, Heather MacIntosh has created a wonderful workbook for adult survivors of complex trauma and their partners. Based on her treatment model, *Development Couple Therapy for Complex Trauma*, this volume provides a detailed set of exercises, ideas, and psychoeducational resources that allow trauma-impacted couples to address their difficulties and challenges at a level not commonly found in books written for survivors. I can't recommend this workbook enough, not only for its compassionate, intelligent stance, but also for its deep and accurate appreciation of the real, everyday experiences of hurt people and those they love. By the way, the illustrations are perfect!"

John Briere, *Ph.D. Author of* Principles of Trauma Therapy:
A Guide to Symptoms, Evaluation, and Treatment

Healing Broken Bonds

This one-of-a-kind theoretical and practical workbook provides couples with tools to work towards healing their relationships and experiences of trauma. It will be an invaluable resource for mental health professionals working with trauma survivors and those who are using Developmental Couple Therapy for Complex Trauma (DCTCT) with the couples they work with.

Serving as a self-help guide for couples as well as a companion to *Developmental Couple Therapy for Complex Trauma: A Manual for Therapists*, this workbook provides couples with accessible exercises they can work with on their own and for clinicians to share with their clients to support their therapy work. Chapters cover psychoeducation, skills building, attachment focused dyadic processing, and consolidation so couples can bring these new skills and insights into daily life. Featuring downloadable handouts and journal reflections, as well as questions and discussion prompts throughout, the author holds in mind the varied backgrounds that patients come from, such as their cultural, ethnic, community, sexual and gender identities, and socio-economic group, and integrates these diverse needs into the exercises, thus providing inclusivity within the treatment process.

The book is essential reading for trauma survivor couples and individuals looking to build stronger and healthier relationships, as well as couple and family therapists, counsellors, and other mental health professionals who help clients navigate experiences of trauma.

Heather B. MacIntosh, Ph.D., is a clinical psychologist and associate professor and Director of the MScA Couple and Family Therapy Programme in the School of Social Work at McGill University. She is the recipient of the H. Noel Fieldhouse Award for Distinguished Teaching.

Healing Broken Bonds

A Couple's Workbook for Complex Trauma

Heather B. MacIntosh, Ph.D.

Routledge
Taylor & Francis Group

NEW YORK AND LONDON

Designed cover image: Kathleen Weldon

First published 2025
by Routledge
605 Third Avenue, New York, NY 10158

and by Routledge
4 Park Square, Milton Park, Abingdon, Oxon, OX14 4RN

Routledge is an imprint of the Taylor & Francis Group, an informa business

ISBN: 978-1-032-36247-2 (hbk)
ISBN: 978-1-032-36246-5 (pbk)
ISBN: 978-1-003-33095-0 (ebk)

DOI: 10.4324/9781003330950

Typeset in Sabon
by Newgen Publishing UK

Access the Support Material: www.routledge.com/9781032362465

This workbook is dedicated to the determination and perseverance of trauma survivors who continue to seek love, connection, light, and closeness, in human relationships in spite of all of the hurt and pain that has made that road such a rocky one.

Contents

Acknowledgements   *xv*

Introduction   1
   Purpose and Format of This Workbook 2
   What Is Developmental Couple Therapy for Complex Trauma (DCTCT)? 2
   Who Am I? 4
   How to Navigate This Workbook 6
   Should You Work Through the Workbook on Your Own or with Your
      Partner? 7

STAGE ONE
Psychoeducation   **9**

1.1 Impacts of Trauma   11
   Handout: How Trauma Impacts Individuals 12
   Journal Reflections: Impacts of Trauma 13
   Journal Reflections Handout: Impacts of Trauma 14

1.2 Impact of Trauma on Couple Relationships   17
   Handout: Impact of Trauma on Couples 17
   Journal Reflections: Impact of Trauma on Couple Relationships 18
   Journal Reflections Handout: Impact of Trauma on Couple
      Relationships 18

1.3 Emotion Regulation   21
   Handout: Emotions and Childhood Trauma 21
   Journal Reflections Handout: Emotion Regulation, Trauma, and
      Couples 24

1.4 Primary and Secondary Emotions   26
   Journal Reflections Handout: Primary and Secondary Emotions 28

1.5   Shame   29
Handout: Shame 30
Journal Reflections Handout: Shame and Your Relationship 32

1.6   Mentalizing   34
Handout: Mentalizing 34
Examples of Mentalizing 37
  Mentalizing Well 37
  Mentalizing Struggles 37
  Takeaways 38
Journal Reflections Handout: Mentalizing 38

1.7   Trauma and Attachment   40
Handout: Trauma and Attachment 40
Journal Reflections Handout: Attachment and Trauma 43

1.8   Negative Cycles and Dyadic Traumatic Reenactment (DTR)   48
Handout: Negative Cycles and Dyadic Traumatic Reenactment 48
Exercise: Identify the Negative Cycle 49
Journal Reflections Handout: Identify the Negative Cycle and DTR 51

1.9   Sex and Sexuality After Trauma   53
Handout: Sex and Sexuality after Trauma 54

1.10 Trauma, the Body, and Sex   56
Journal Reflections: Trauma, Sex, and Sexuality 56
Journal Reflections Handout: Trauma, Sex, and Sexuality 57

STAGE TWO
Building Capacity   **61**

2.1   Skills Building in Emotion Regulation   63
Moving into Working Together and Consent 64
Exercise: Square Breathing 65
Journal Reflections Handout: Square Breathing 67

2.2   Naming Emotions   69
Exercise: Name That Feeling! 70
  Step One: Identifying and Naming Primary Feelings 70
  Step Two: Identifying and Naming More Complex Feelings 72
  Step Three: Expanding Feelings 73
  Step Four: Sharing Your Feelings 75
  Adding to the Challenge 75
Journal Reflections Handout: Name That Feeling! 76

Exercise: Exploring Learned Emotional Relationships 77
Journal Reflections Handout: Learned Emotional Relationships 78

2.3 Moving into Co-regulation   80
Journal Reflections Handout: Co-regulation 80
Beginning to Put It Together 81
Exercise: Dyadic Emotional Coping, Initial Exploration 81
Exercise: Dyadic Emotional Coping, Deeper Exploration 82

2.4 Regulation and Rhythm   86
Exercise: Regulation and Rhythm: Individual 86
  Step One: Finding Regulation 86
  Step Two: Regulating 87
Journal Reflections Handout: Regulation and Rhythm: Individual 87
Exercise: Regulation and Rhythm: Dyadic 88
  Step One: Creating Space 89
  Step Two: Sharing a Song 89
Journal Reflections Handout: Regulation and Rhythm: Dyadic 90
Expanding into the Youness 91

2.5 Skills Building in Mentalizing   92
Journal Reflections Handout: How Do I Understand Mentalizing? 92
Imagining the Inside from the Outside 94
Journal Reflections Handout: Imagining the Inside from the Outside 95
Exercise: Adopting a Mentalizing Stance 96
  Step One: Small Stakes, Big Learnings 96
  Step Two: Sharing Perspectives 96
  Step Three: Receiving Perspectives 97
  Step Four: Tag, You're It! 97
Journal Reflections Handout: Adopting a Mentalizing Stance in a Low
  Stakes Role Play 98
Mentalizing Skill Building Exercise 100
Mentalizing Skill Building Handout 100
Mentalizing Skill Building Cheat Sheet 104
Mentalizing Cheat Sheet Handout 104
Orienting to Mentalizing 105
A Final Note About Stage Two 105

STAGE THREE
Attachment-Focused Dyadic Processing   **109**

3.1 Attachment Histories Living in the Present   111
Review 111
Journal Reflections Handout: Review 111

How Do We Change Our Attachment Styles and Build Earned
   Security? 112
   Survivor Couple Attachment Styles 112
   How Did We Get Here? 113
Journal Reflections Handout: Your Attachment Style 115
Consistency and Change 118
Journal Reflections Handout: Consistency and Change 118
Making the Unconscious Conscious 119
Journal Reflections Handout: Consistency of Attachment 120
The Change Part! Introducing Secure Base Behaviours 121
Journal Reflections Handout: Secure Base Behaviours Chart 125
Exercise: Secure Base Behaviours 128
   First Run Through 129
   Step One: Identifying the Weak Link in the Sequence 129
Secure Base Behaviours Exercise Step One: Identifying the Weak Link in
   the Sequence Handout 129
   Step Two: Identifying the Link to Early Development 133
Secure Base Behaviour Exercise Step Two: Identifying the Link to Early
   Development Handout 134
   Step Three: Strategies for Change 139

3.2   Disclosure: Telling the Stories   141
Disclosing Beyond the Title of the Story 141
Disclosing The Title of Your Trauma Story Handout 142
Going Deeper and Growing Closer 144
Exercise: Setting the Stage for Telling the Story 145
   Step One: Disclosures Begin 146
Disclosure Exercise Step One: Disclosures Begin 146
   Step Two: Part One: Disclosures That Remain 149
Disclosure Exercise Step Two: Part One: Disclosures That Remain 149
   Step Two: Part Two: Preparation for Partner 152
Disclosure Exercise Step Two: Part Two: Preparation for Partner 152
   Step Three: The Sharing 154
Other Kinds of Secrets 157
Journal Reflections Handout: Other Kinds of Secrets 158

3.3   Trauma Processing in a Dyadic Context   161
Journal Reflections Handout: Traumatic Memories and Your
   Relationship 165
Traumatic Memory Processing 167
Exercise: List of Triggers Handout 168
Sharing 168

Journal Reflections: For Partners 169
Journal Reflections Handout: For Partners 169
Making a List Together 170
Exercise: Making a List Together Handout 171
Journal Reflections: How Are We Changing? 173
Journal Reflections Handout: How Are We Changing? 173

3.4   Sex and Sexuality   176
Culture, Family, and Sex for Survivors 177
Journal Reflections Handout: Family, Culture, and Sex 177
Our Traumatized, Embodied, Sexual Selves 180
Journal Reflections Handout: Our Relationship with Our Body 181
It's All About Consent and Communication 184
As They Say—You've Got to Love Yourself First! 185
Exercise: Finding Your Way to Your Own Sexual Body 186
  Step One: Mental Body Scan 186
  Step Two: Felt Body Scan 186
  Step Three: Exploratory Self-Touch 187
  Step Four: Moving Towards Orgasm 187
Exercise: Finding Your Way to Your Own Sexual Body Handout 188
Journal Reflections: Finding Your Sexuality 190
Journal Reflections Handout: Finding Your Sexuality 190
Navigating Triggers 192
Decreasing Sexual Secrets 195
Journal Reflections Handout: Sexual Secrets 197
Journal Reflections Handout: Sharing Sexual Secrets 202
Reducing Bifurcation 204
Breaking the Seal 205

3.5   Dyadic Traumatic Reenactment   209
Journal Reflections: DTRs 209
Journal Reflections Handout: Dyadic Traumatic Reenactment 210
Working Through the DTRs Together 213
Exercise: Noticing and Naming 215
Exercise: Noticing and Naming Handout 215
Exercise: Accepting and Acknowledging 217
Exercise: Accepting and Acknowledging Handout 218
Exercise: Catching and Changing 219
Exercise: Catching and Changing Handout 220
Exercise: DTR Worksheet 223

STAGE FOUR
Consolidation

225

4.1   Consolidation   227
      Checklist for Pulling It All Together 228

      Index   *232*

Acknowledgements

To the students, research assistants, therapists, and the couples themselves, who have brought all of themselves to the task of learning more about how trauma lives in us, our relationships, and how we can heal. Without you, this landscape would be a lonely one.

The research upon which this workbook is built has been supported by the Fund for Assistance to Victims of Criminal Acts (Fond d'aide aux victimes d'actes criminels; FAVAC) of the Government of Quebec, the Social Sciences and Humanities Research Council, and the Fonds de recherche du Québec société et culture.

Research Team

Research Assistants: Miles Cooke, Aicha Farhat, Jackson Hagner, Ainsley Jenicek, Sarah McNamee, Emilie Marzinotto, Jamie Zarn

Interns: Nadia Argueta, Ojasvi Bhardwaj, Jélénia Cyrise, Cayley Deane, Claire Gregor, Jackson Hagner, Tawnie Lahache, ME Louis, Verity Ly, Frédrique MacDougall, Sarah McNamee, Krishna Makhania, Myrlie Marcelin, Emilie Marzinotto, Kae Parker, Jamie Zarn

Therapists: Sarah Burley, Jackson Hagner, Ainsley Jenicek, Stephen Legari, Heather B. MacIntosh, Rachel Starr, Sèdami Gwladys Tossa

Consultant: Melissa Jacobs Swamp

Illustrations

Kathleen Weldon

Copy Editing

P. Rose Primeau

Introduction

It is impossible to find the right words to welcome you here. I know that you have found this "place" because you are seeking support and strategies for a challenging journey. So, perhaps, it is simply that I am glad that you have found this workbook, and I hope it helps you get one step closer to the kind of loving, close, safe, and comforting relationship you desire and deserve.

Healing Broken Bonds, the title of this workbook, may have spoken to you as you continue to throw a lifeline to a relationship that is drowning, struggling to come up for air over and over again, filled with pain, and threatening to go under. Perhaps the title drew you in because you have done the same thing over and over again in your relationships and you just can't find your way to something new and different that feels safe, loving, and lasting. Perhaps you picked this book up off the shelf because you have never been able to have a relationship at all, because the very thought of letting yourself trust, open up, and expose yourself to another person is beyond terrifying. Whatever the reasons, you are here: opening these pages, hoping for help, support, and resources to improve your relationships and build safety and closeness to weather the storms of life and come through them stronger.

It is also possible that you have found your way to these pages because your therapist is working through the process of Developmental Couple Therapy for Complex Trauma (DCTCT) with you and your partner, and they suggested that you follow along. Whatever the reason you picked up this workbook, it is my hope that we can journey along together, you, your partner(s),[1] and me, to explore some of the struggles of what it means to be a trauma survivor trying to live, love, and heal in relationships.

However you got here, we've found one another across a crowded room of self-help books. If you are anything like me, you have a bookshelf full of books that you imagined would help you sleep better, feel better, concentrate better, eat better, and, well, simply be better. And yet, if you are also anything like me, you've come up feeling like you know more, but you are still searching for something that will help you feel better in your bones and in your relational self. I hope that through the pages of this book you will be able to both learn more knowledge, build more skills, and imagine new ways of being: through trying some of the exercises, engaging with the journaling, and dialoguing with your therapist, partner, friends, and others close to you.

DOI: 10.4324/9781003330950-1

Purpose and Format of This Workbook

This workbook follows the four stages of the DCTCT approach to couple therapy. Each section takes you through the information that can help you understand some aspect of how experiences of trauma may be impacting you, your partner, and your relationship. Along with the information is a selection of exercises and journal prompts that may help you move along.

We are all busy in our lives with work and families, and those of us living with the impacts of trauma in our lives may have less bandwidth for extras, even if they are good extras.

To get the most out of the workbook, try to be as committed and consistent as you can tolerate and as is reasonable given the realities of your life. When working with me, some couples set up a date night for doing any exercises or journal reflections, a routine that stays the same every week. Other couples take a look at their schedules and identify a time to come together during the week between our sessions. Whatever works best for you will be the strategy that will bring you the most success. I certainly don't want you to end up having conflict about working through exercises designed to help you have less conflict! However, finding a designated time and space for working on these exercises and reflections makes a real difference to you making your way through the parts of the workbook that will help you and your partner find your way through the tangled web that is love after trauma.

What Is Developmental Couple Therapy for Complex Trauma (DCTCT)?

DCTCT is an approach to couple therapy with trauma survivors that I developed over many years of research and clinical practice. During my doctoral studies, I worked with Dr. Sue Johnson on research with childhood sexual abuse survivors in Emotionally Focused Therapy (EFT) for couples.[2] From this research, I learned that survivors can really struggle in their relationships and in the therapy process itself. I have spent the last fifteen years specifically working on developing an approach to couple therapy that could help trauma survivors with the impacts of their own traumas on their own selves, with the impacts of traumas on the couple, and on the actual process of therapy, to help survivors feel understood, and to help build the kinds of skills and knowledge necessary to tolerate and benefit from the therapy.

Specifically, there are things that happen as we develop through life that build up the capacities that are necessary for developing and maintaining close, safe, and loving couple relationships. These capacities can be damaged or never have a chance to develop when we experience traumas, especially when those traumas occur in childhood. So, as we move through life, we may find that we get into the same difficulties over and over again—like high conflict, high intensity, relationships that become hot and heavy very quickly but then end just as quickly with a bang. We may struggle with things like traumatic stress symptoms, emotion regulation challenges, and difficulties with something called mentalizing, which we will explore in depth as we move along through the book. These challenges make it hard to navigate the daily challenges of relationships, normal conflicts, supporting and caring for one another, receiving care and support, and so many important facets of being connected to a partner. These same challenges also have an impact on being able to tolerate and benefit from couple therapy.

There are many solid and effective approaches to couple therapy, but they all rest on the assumption that the participants can *do* the tasks of the therapy. For many trauma survivors, the very things that make it hard for them to navigate being in a couple relationship are the same things that make it hard to *do* the tasks of the therapy and to tolerate and benefit from couple therapy. DCTCT was developed out of my growing understanding that when couples, and the individuals within those couples, are dealing with trauma, they need to have support in building up these important capacities so that they can *do* the tasks of the therapy and, eventually, *do* the tasks of loving and being loved, navigating the normal conflicts and stresses of couple life, being close, feeling safe and connected, and generally feeling like this relationship is a place where trauma has been left behind and we are safe to live, love, laugh, and just be with a partner who can do and be us.

That is how Developmental Couple Therapy for Complex Trauma was born. Therapists have found the original treatment manual to be helpful in their work with survivor couples, but it isn't written in a way that would be helpful to the couples themselves as they move through the stages. This workbook was conceived with survivor couples in mind.

Stage One of DCTCT focuses on helping you and your partner come to a shared understanding of what it means to be trauma survivors in relationships. We will explore the impacts of trauma on individuals and couples, and other important topics including:

Why do my emotions feel so terrifying and out of control?
Why is it hard for me to hold on to my partner in my mind when I am distressed?
What happens to my partner and I when we get sucked into a vortex that just doesn't make sense, but we can't find our way out?
Why can I never feel safe with them?
What makes it so hard for us to resolve conflicts, have great sex, and feel confident in our relationship?

Stage Two of DCTCT focuses on building new skills and strategies to tolerate and manage emotions, even when life in the present is on a crash course with trauma from the past. We will also focus on learning how to build and sustain the ability to hold our partner in mind even when we are distressed and feeling stuck in trauma-land. Holding onto our own minds and selves as life swirls around us can be one of the biggest challenges we face as trauma survivors, when we get triggered by the pull of the past as it intrudes into our relationships. Sometimes we can feel like it is all threatening to take our minds along with the stress and conflict of daily life.

These first two stages are important to set you up for success in navigating the third stage of DCTCT.

Stage Three of DCTCT is where we get into the bread and butter of how trauma is living in your relationship. The first step in this stage is sharing our stories. So often our partners know the "title" but don't know what's in the book. They know that there was abuse or trauma, but they don't really know what happened. In our work with survivor couples, the ones who are able to share their stories—and support one another in working through how these traumas are still alive and kicking—are the couples that came through therapy more satisfied and closer together. We then dive into how your struggles with trauma may be intruding in very real ways like flashbacks and nightmares, and in other less obvious ways like cycles that repeat echoes of your trauma stories in the same, recurring argument. We also explore how your sexual relationship is affected by trauma and how couples can heal those wounds together. And, in some ways most importantly, we work on how your ability to attach and feel secure with one another has been affected by trauma so you can try some strategies for building safety and closeness, something called "earned secure attachment", together.

Stage Four of DCTCT focuses on what we call consolidation—bringing all of the knowledge and skills, earned attachment security, and the safety and confidence that comes from working through past and present traumas together to face daily life as a couple. In this stage we apply all of the hard work and learning that you have done in the first three stages to situations as they occur: conflicts, challenges, crises, and change.

Trust yourself. You can start at the end and work your way back, cherry pick based on your curiosity, and trust your intuition about what will work for you when. If you have survived traumas, found your way into relationships that are important to you, and found your way to this workbook: trust yourself, you have a lot going for you. You will have developed capacities to survive; that some of these are areas of strength will mean that you can skip over sections that do not feel necessary for you. Follow the order and pace that feels right for you.

Who Am I?

If we are going to go on this journey together, you might want to know a little bit about your tour guide. If you're someone who likes a little mystery, feel free to skip this bit.

I spent the first six months of my life in foster care. This is a dark empty space, being in the care of people mandated by the state to care for you, before you have words or memory. I was then adopted into a family that didn't understand how trauma might impact a tiny human, and they were living their own intergenerational nightmares that were oozing their way down the family tree like sticky sap, untapped and uncontrollable. What I learned of family, loyalty, love, and life was only that it's amazing what you can survive and still have desire, hope, and longing for love.

We now understand that bodies hold imprints of trauma, even before words and memory are possible, but that was not known or understood at the time I wrestled my way through the early part of my life. Even moving into adulthood, parenthood, and relationships, knowing something was wrong but never being able to put words, images, or stories to the embodied resurfacings of my earliest traumas, it was difficult to be fully alive in my daily existence. While I started out as a musician, a singer, that embodiment of trauma also had its tentacles on my muscles, joints, and bones; we relive the trauma in somatic-embodied memories, but we also carry the physical scars of the "actual" damage done to tiny human bodies. My career as a classical singer was cut short due to both the *psyche* and the *soma* (the mind and the body). Something that had felt like a consolation prize for all of the misery, my ability to find myself truly immersed in the music and to feel the joy and the torment of the songs, was lost. I wondered how I could possibly find meaning in a life where the one thing that made me, well, me—and that had been the melody of my survival—was lost.

I spent years searching for something that could help me understand what had happened, and what was continuing to happen, to me. I worked in jobs as a medical secretary, music teacher, church soloist and music director, waitress, typist, and babysitter, and even as a singing balloonagram clown. I took one course at a time, first to finish high school, and then to start university; I just kept searching for a way to understand my own struggles and to find meaning in a life that no longer made sense.

That search led me to reading many of the authors who were starting to write about and help folks understand trauma. I read my way through volumes of journals, every book I could find on trauma, and I began volunteering to help researchers who were starting to study childhood trauma, sexual abuse, traumatic memory, and how survivors survive. I started to see that my life could have meaning as part of this growing force making sense of the senseless violence inflicted on children by those who should protect them. From there, the course was fairly steady. I supported myself as a musician as I pursued studies in music and psychology, and, after many years and many sleepless nights working multiple jobs to support myself and my two children, I completed a doctorate in clinical psychology.

My clinical life started when I worked in a rape crisis centre on the 24-hour crisis line. Over and over, I heard stories of violence, abuse, and abandonment, and I was struck by the immensity of people's capacity for survival. As I began working as a therapist with individuals and, eventually, with couples and families, my interest in trauma continued to grow and with it grew an immense respect and awe for how people survive atrocities and strive to build loving relationships, despite having experienced the worst that humanity has to offer.

My work is influenced by my personal life: clearly, by my own traumas, but also through my struggles to navigate being a mother and a partner, having had very few experiences of positive parenting and finding very few examples of positive partnering as models. I am a queer and gender non-conforming human, and I have been in a loving, monogamous relationship for 27 years with Pat: another musician, social worker, mother, and all-around good human. Learning how to show up, not be a jerk, do the dishes more often than I would like, express my anger and frustration, share my grief and nightmares, and be there for her as we traverse the fun and frolic of growing old together, has been the biggest challenge of my survivorship—you just don't get the manual for loving relationships when you grow up in a great big morass of humans not showing up for you.

Although I have faced significant obstacles based on loss, trauma, and queer identity, I am white and grew up in a middle class, suburban community. My differences were invisible, and I was never held back from opportunity by the colour of my skin, my last name, or my postal code. I am really only learning now about how trauma for black, brown, Indigenous, and trans people, and the unhoused and those living in precarious situations, is rampant in the everyday movements of their lives. Racism, transphobia, colonialism, and discrimination at all levels compounds experiences of childhood traumas; how can you work on feeling safe if, in fact, you are not? So much of the writing about recovering from trauma is built upon an assumption of danger then, safety now, which is simply not true for many survivors. My voice is a white voice, and I am working to be an ally to other less-represented voices. And yet, I know that there will be ways in which this workbook misses, fails, and flails, when it comes to addressing the needs of all survivors; I encourage you to reach out and let me know, to reach out to members of your own communities to share your stories, and to continue to seek safety in spaces where that is possible.

At this point in my life, I divide my time between teaching, research, and supervision in the master's programme in Couple and Family Therapy at McGill University in Montreal, Quebec, Canada, and MerryMac Farm, my lovely farm in North Lancaster, Ontario, Canada. On our farm we have an ever-revolving door of barn cats; Molly, Calvin, and Ruby, the kune kune pigs; Hnaggur, Fjóla, Sigla, Spá, and Perla, the Icelandic horses; Sassy, the mini mule, and Titan, the miniature horse; Bear and Mae, the Great Pyrenees dogs; and an ever-changing number of Icelandic chickens. All of these creatures share my 40 acres of trails and reforested farmland. It is here that my body and spirit has been learning what it means to feel alive, whole, and free. It is here that I have learned about rhythm, that you rise with the sun, that the animals need feeding at regular intervals, that that happens every day, and that they put themselves to bed when they are tired, play when they are feeling playful, and seek comfort when they are hurt. I have witnessed birth and death, and all of the ways that nature tells us about itself. I did not know, before these animals walked me through a thousand days and nights, about rhythms—simply listening to a body, the signals that nature gives us, and responding with eating, drinking, sleeping, and loving, with loving as vital as all the rest.

It is not easy for a body that was born into chaos and pain to shift focus into beauty, grace, and rhythm—it can be a battle from moment to moment, hour to hour, and day to day, but when I walk back to the house on a crisp fall night, and look up into the dark night sky and see the constellations shining down on me, I remember to breathe deeply and just notice, for a while, that the expanse of the world around me is much larger than anything that was ever done to me. And then, I go back into the house, Pat and I share stories of our day as she rubs my feet, and I fix the remote control that is messing with our ability to watch Netflix.

I do not wish for you miracles. Neither do I wish for you magic. What I wish for you is ease, contentment more often than torment, and gentleness more often than self-hatred. I wish for you to find rhythms that bring you back into relationship with yourself, your body, your partner, and your living. If this workbook can help you, I will feel that some of my experiences have found their way to become meaningful.

How to Navigate This Workbook

While this book is organized in stages that follow the stages of the DCTCT model of couple therapy, you may find yourself drawn to certain sections that reflect something that is happening in your relationship right now, and it is okay to do some hopping around as you navigate your way through the book. However, the first two stages are designed to help you with the third stage. It can be very challenging to work through traumatic memories, work on your sexuality and sexual relationship, and share your stories of abuse and neglect with a partner; having the understanding and skills from the first and second stages of DCTCT can help.

In the years since the original book was published (2019), my wonderful team of research assistants, students, and community therapists have done a lot more clinical research with couples dealing with the impacts of trauma on their relationships. Based on these experiences, I have reordered and expanded the psychoeducational materials in the Stage One section of this workbook to be more cohesive and to follow the developmental path we are building together. If you are following along with your DCTCT therapist, in the workbook, you and your therapist can decide together the order that will best work for you and your partner.

I have no doubt that you know all about being triggered, activated, overwhelmed, or whatever word you use for being thrown into feeling like trauma is happening right here, right now. However, it's certainly not a barrel of laughs, and sometimes it can feel like everything is falling apart, inside and out, while we are trying so hard to pull it all together. The first two sections of the book are designed to help you find ways to manage those moments of being triggered into overwhelming feelings and memories that intrude uninvited. As you read through those first two stages and try out the exercises in the second stage, keep track of which strategies and exercises help you come back into yourself, your body, mind, and spirit, and bookmark those for easy access when you need them as you work your way through the parts of the book that are more challenging for you.

If you need to put the workbook down and come back, it's okay. If you need to take a break, it's okay: trust yourself and pace yourself. One thing we know very clearly, from all the research into trauma over the last thirty years, is that forcing, pushing, flooding, and dissociating, while trying to work through memories and overwhelming experiences, just leads to more distress and doesn't actually resolve anything. The take-home message is, less is more—if we aren't in a pretty settled space, the work is harder and less effective.

Should You Work Through the Workbook on Your Own or with Your Partner?

This book is primarily about helping couples who are dealing with the impacts of trauma on their relationships. There are many parts of the book that will invite you to work on an activity or exercise on your own while other exercises and activities will focus on practising a skill or way of being with your partner. If you are in a relationship with someone who you feel you can share the exercises and activities with: that's great, go for it. If you are not, that's also okay. Whatever way you can make your way through the learning, trying, and working through, is okay. What matters is that you are working on your *self*, your trauma, and your relationships—past, present, and future. How ever you arrive here is okay.

Notes

1 For the purposes of ease I will use the word partner, in the singular, knowing that many survivors of trauma find their way to safety, empowerment, and joy in polyamorous and consensually non-monogamous relationship systems.
2 This work resulted in the article: MacIntosh, H. B., & Johnson, S. (2008). Emotionally focused therapy for couples and childhood sexual abuse survivors. *Journal of Marital and Family Therapy*, 34(3), 298–315.

Psychoeducation

Stage one includes a series of handouts that cover each topic. These handouts are resources from the DCTCT treatment manual that your DCTCT therapist will be using if you have a therapist you are working with. However, as we have spent more time with couples in the intervening years since the manual was written, I have made some additions and changes so the handouts aren't necessarily the same as those in the treatment manual.

All the handouts in this book are available for download at www.routledge.com/9781032362465.

DOI: 10.4324/9781003330950-2

Impacts of Trauma

I have a vivid memory, from about 20 years ago, when I first started working with couples who were dealing with the impacts of trauma on their relationships. This was my first research study, and the title was pretty clear—couple therapy and childhood sexual abuse—not much was left to the imagination, or so you'd think. A young couple called and asked to participate in the research project, so we invited them to the clinic to meet with me and fill in some questionnaires to help us learn more about what they were living, in both their lives and their relationship.

Before meeting couples, we don't know if they are "single" or "dual" trauma couples. Do both partners have experiences of trauma in their backgrounds, or it is just one partner? For this reason, we ask both partners to fill out the same questionnaires and some of the questions are related to how traumas may be lurking in the life of the survivor. In this case, it was a single trauma, straight, cisgender couple, with the woman reporting that she experienced sexual abuse in childhood.

As the couple was completing the questionnaires, the male partner got to the question about posttraumatic stress disorder. He started responding far more slowly to the questions. I kept a pretty close eye on him as he seemed to be growing more and more distressed.

After completing about half of the questions he looked up at me and asked, "Is this what she is going through?" His partner was sitting right there, but he looked like the world had swallowed him whole, pulling him into a vortex of unknowable devastation. I reassured him that she may be going through those things, and that was part of what our work would be—to help him understand her experiences more fully and to help them find ways to communicate and connect more deeply, securely, and safely. The look on his face seemed to be a contorted combination of grief, horror, rage, and torment; he simply did not know that the person he loved was living this nightmare. This couple is not alone. This is a common story I have seen over and over through the years of my work with trauma survivor couples.

The first step then, in coming together and healing together is to build a shared understanding of what is happening. Being able to see this problem—trauma—as an entity outside of your love and commitment, helps many couples to work together on their relationship, turning towards one another rather than turning away and falling into blame and anger. And the first step in this is really building a strong and shared understanding of what trauma is and what trauma does. In the following section you will find handouts,

DOI: 10.4324/9781003330950-3

exercises, and journal reflection prompts to help you, as an individual, and as a couple, to begin to downgrade hurricane *Trauma* to tropical storm *We're getting there* and, eventually, to calm summer day on the lake.

HANDOUT: HOW TRAUMA IMPACTS INDIVIDUALS

What is trauma?

- A traumatic event is an overwhelming or uncontrollable experience that can happen to anyone at any age.
- It may be a life-threatening experience or may involve witnessing something that causes you to feel horrified, helpless, or intensely fearful for your life or the lives of others.
- Traumatic events can include child abuse, domestic violence/partner violence, combat violence, sudden/unexpected loss of a loved one, a car accident, sexual abuse/violence, and natural disasters (e.g., hurricanes).
- Some traumas are common in childhood, such as sexual, physical, and emotional abuse and neglect.
- Some traumas are more common in adulthood, such as conjugal violence, car accidents, natural disasters, and assaults.

How might trauma impact you?

- **Sense of self**: you may experience feelings of helplessness, shame, guilt, self-blame, feeling "not normal", altered sense of age.
- **Memory and perception**: you may also experience memory problems, dissociation (feeling outside of your body, losing time, not feeling real).
- **Sense of meaning**: you may experience loss of faith, despair, feeling that you do not have a future, a sense of hopelessness.
- **Relationships**: you may experience revictimization, isolation, difficulty maintaining close relationships due to mistrust, difficulty with resolving conflicts, difficulty sharing secrets, and tend towards viewing others as rescuers/victims/aggressors, with repetition of problematic relationship patterns.
- **Physical well-being**: you may experience difficulties with sleep, disordered eating, substance abuse issues, and/or other health problems that have been associated with a history of trauma.
- **Emotional well-being**: you may have difficulty tolerating and experiencing challenging emotions, including anxiety, sadness, and anger; you may alternate between feelings of numbness (no feelings) and being out of control (too much feeling).

How is childhood trauma different?

- Childhood trauma occurs during periods of important development of social, emotional, cognitive, and physical growth.
- Overwhelming or uncontrollable experiences can happen to anyone at any age.
- However, when trauma occurs in childhood, impacts can be more severe and long-lasting because the trauma has an impact on your overall development.
- It often happens in the context of relationships where the person who hurts you is also the person who is supposed to take care of you.

Trauma and identity past and present

- Trauma lives in our minds and bodies across time, like an imprint of a hand in the sand; it wears away over time, but that imprint stays deep in the memory of the sand. Even when trauma has happened in the past we can still feel as though it is happening right now. To heal, there needs to be enough safe open space for our minds and bodies to settle and allow those imprints to start to dissipate. However, for many of us, trauma continues to happen in new and different forms.
- Childhood trauma survivors are at high risk of experiencing dangerous levels of conflict and violence in their couple relationships.
- Childhood trauma survivors are also at a high risk of experiencing sexual assault and sexual traumas in adulthood.
- For LGBTQ+ persons, daily experiences of homophobia and transphobia can magnify the impacts of past trauma, retraumatizing us over and over again and keeping old traumas from having a chance to settle and resolve.
    - The messages coming at us from individuals and from society, telling us that to be queer, to be trans, to be different, are an assault on that very sense of self and our comfort in relationships that may already be compromised by earlier traumas.
    - Both homophobia and transphobia, and the ways in which families and communities can reject and alienate us, can be sources of new traumas that conspire with our historical traumas to inflate the impacts of both past and present wounds.
- For BIPOC persons, daily experiences of racism, colonization, and unrelenting discrimination can also magnify the impacts of past trauma, adding more of a heavy load as past and present traumas collide.
    - And it's important to remember that, for many of us, our identities—BIPOC, queer, trans, fat, disabled, among others—can all be ways in which the world, and the people in it, find to target us as children and lay the foundation for internalized feelings of self hatred; trauma can tell us that we are, in essence, bad. Identity-based trauma can tell us that, on top of our "basic" bad, we are also bad because we are queer, trans, black, brown, fat, neurodivergent, disabled, etc.
- In our fractured world it is becoming more common, again, to be assaulted and assailed by violence for our identities—racial, religious, sexual orientation and gender identity, among so many others. For many of us, it is impossible to leave trauma in the past when it feels so present on a daily basis.
- The impacts of cumulative trauma are cumulative. These cumulative traumas, especially when targeted around our identities, are, at times, socially sanctioned forms of trauma that reinforce the beliefs that grow up around us when the people who are meant to protect us cause us harm.

Journal Reflections: Impacts of Trauma

For this first journaling activity, I would suggest you do it on your own, at least at first. Even if you are reading this section with your partner, take a break and find a private, quiet space, if that is possible, to reflect on the nature of your own traumas, how they are affecting you now, and how you see them infiltrating your life. If, once you have given yourself lots of time to reflect and write, it feels possible to share them with your partner, go for it.

Thinking about how trauma can thrust itself into the present, I would also invite you to reflect on how aspects of your life, relationships, and identity can mean that there is no rest from "past" trauma when "present" traumas still lurk, waiting to pounce.

For this to be healing and helping, ask yourself, am I breathing, thinking, feeling, sensing, in my body, in my mind, and not too activated or numbed out? If you answer yes to the majority of these, you can proceed. If you answer no to the majority of these, take a break. Do something that will bring you back into your body and come back to the exercise when you are feeling more settled and present.

JOURNAL REFLECTIONS HANDOUT: IMPACTS OF TRAUMA

What kinds of traumas would you say that you have experienced? (This is not the space to write the details—more about the titles to the stories.)

_____

_____

_____

_____

_____

_____

Where do you see yourself in the descriptions of the impacts of trauma?

_____

_____

_____

_____

_____

_____

Are there aspects of your identities that are a source of trauma and oppression in your life in the present?

_____

_____

_____

_____

_____

_____

Which impacts would you say are having the biggest influence on your inner life?

_____

_____

_____

_____

_____

_____

Which impacts would you say are having the biggest influence on your relationship life?

_____

_____

_____

_____

_____

_____

How have you found what works for you in managing these impacts?

_____

_____

_____

_____

_____

_____

How have you coped with the impacts of trauma on your life? How effective were these strategies? Did these strategies work long term?

_____

_____

_____

_____

_____

_____

_____

What feels resolved in terms of your work on your personal trauma and the impacts on your relationship?

_____

_____

_____

_____

_____

_____

What continues to linger in terms of your work on your personal trauma and the impacts on your relationship?

_____

_____

_____

_____

_____

_____

Impact of Trauma on Couple Relationships

It's a long walk from the inside to the outside. As we come to learn more about how trauma affects us it is natural to think about the "inside": those parts of ourselves that are, perhaps, less visible, like our thoughts and feelings, nightmares and memories, sense of self, and whether we can feel safe in our own selves, let alone with others.

These inside impacts are huge and sometimes we keep ourselves so busy that the "outside" gets lost in the sweep of our own internal turmoil. When we can be settled, soothed, and quiet enough on the inside, we can be present for what the outside brings. Sometimes this is a really challenging, painful process. When our inside lives are so full of pain and compelling, traumatic memories and states, it can be really hard to pay attention to our relationships on the outside.

Trauma survivors, especially those of us who experienced trauma in childhood at the hands of people who should have protected us, often have a really hard time in all kinds of relationships—as parents, friends, partners, and even colleagues.

When looking specifically at couple relationships there are a few specific areas of challenge that stand out. These include impacts on trust, closeness, sexuality, emotion regulation, empathy, and communication.

HANDOUT: IMPACT OF TRAUMA ON COUPLES

How might childhood trauma affect your couple relationships?

- **Trust**: When people are traumatized in childhood, especially by people close to them, this can impact their ability to trust their partners in adulthood. Survivors can tuck themselves away from their partners to protect themselves from being hurt, from opening up and risking betrayal or abandonment. There are so many ways that lacking in the capacity to trust someone to protect and love us can make it hard to let anyone close.
- **Closeness**: Because you may feel that being close to others has been the source of pain and trauma, being close to your partner in adulthood may feel frightening and dangerous. Often, childhood trauma survivors avoid closeness and, in so doing, become alienated and isolated from their partners. Childhood trauma can lead to high levels of self-criticism, all of which can make it very difficult for childhood trauma survivors to share and feel close to their partners. And, dealing with all of the "inside" impacts of trauma can also lead to secrets—secrets about how we cope,

DOI: 10.4324/9781003330950-4

what we need to do to survive—and the need to keep these secrets can hold us apart from our loved ones.

- **Sexuality**: Because childhood trauma occurs during periods of developmental growth, including sexual development, trauma can impact a person's capacity to feel comfortable in their sexuality. Sexual abuse, especially when perpetrated by someone close to you, can make it difficult to enjoy sex and sexuality in your couple relationship. Certain sexual positions, feelings, and even just being sexually aroused may bring up intense fear/anxiety and provoke flashbacks or vivid reminders of abuse.
- **Emotion regulation and empathy**: Childhood trauma can make it very difficult to understand, feel, and tolerate your emotions and those of your partner. This can mean that when you or your partner are feeling upset and need one another, it may be very difficult for you to tolerate these feelings, to understand the feelings of your partner, and sometimes, to even think in the presence of your own or your partner's distress. Sometimes, when feelings are too big and our partners need us, we can fall into deep, deep pits of shame about how hard it is for us to give our partners what they need. That shame can obliterate any kind of being present with or even being able to see, what our partner needs.
- **Communication**: Childhood trauma survivors often have significant difficulties with communication. As a child, being assertive, clear, and honest may have been dangerous or the information you shared might have been used against you. This may make it very difficult for you to talk to your partner about challenges and conflicts, and sometimes, even everyday things like domestic tasks and childcare become a challenge.

Journal Reflections: Impact of Trauma on Couple Relationships

For this journaling exercise, spend some time with your partner talking and reflecting about the ways in which you can see trauma impacting your couple relationship. If things are feeling too hot or painful, it's okay to reflect on these questions on your own and then share your responses with your partner.

JOURNAL REFLECTIONS HANDOUT: IMPACT OF TRAUMA ON COUPLE RELATIONSHIPS

Where do you, as a couple, see the impacts of trauma on your relationship?

_____

_____

_____

_____

_____

_____

_____

Do you find that conflicts about everyday things feel overwhelming and hard to manage?

_____

_____

_____

_____

_____

_____

What was your relationship like at the beginning?

_____

_____

_____

_____

_____

_____

How has your relationship changed over time?

_____

_____

_____

_____

_____

_____

How have you coped with the challenges you have faced in relation to the impact of your traumas on your relationship? How effective were these strategies? Did these strategies work long term?

_____

_____

_____

_____

_____

_____

_____

Emotion Regulation

Emotion regulation challenges are one of the most significant impacts of developmental trauma and, trauma in general. Our capacity to regulate our emotions—meaning that we can feel them, understand them, learn from them, and even tolerate and manage them—is vital to our relational being. I'm sure you can relate to feeling like you are hanging in there in a conflict or challenging discussion and then, it just becomes too much and, poof—off you go, either into total shut down or into overwhelming floods of intolerable emotional intensity. When we grow up in a loving home and experience all of the developmental supports we require from our caregivers, our ability to identify, feel, tolerate, and learn from our emotions just grows naturally. Our caregivers respond to our feelings, they try to understand them, they try to meet the needs that are expressed in our feelings, and, over time, they show us—from the outside—that our feelings are helpful for being in relationships and managing the big wide world. When we experience trauma, especially trauma in our relationships with our caregivers, those developmental steps either don't happen or they get smashed by the overwhelming impacts of trauma on our psyches and selves.

HANDOUT: EMOTIONS AND CHILDHOOD TRAUMA

Trauma and your emotions

- For survivors of childhood trauma, feelings can sometimes *feel* dangerous, out of control, or confusing. Often survivors have difficulty naming or understanding their feelings, tolerating feelings that may *feel* overwhelming and frightening, and then managing those feelings in ways that would allow them to feel strong, capable, and safe.
- However, feelings are important—emotions give us information! It is essential that survivors start to really understand that emotions serve an important purpose. Emotions give us information about situations, ourselves, and others, and they help us decide what to do in our lives and our relationships.
- Emotions can be uncomfortable, but they are always "healthy". They do not last forever, and we *are not* our emotions. Emotions are simply information messages. We can control our behaviour regardless of the emotions we might be feeling. For instance, you might feel very anxious about asking your partner for a hug when you are feeling insecure. However, that anxiety is just a message from inside of you telling you that this is something you feel some worry about.

DOI: 10.4324/9781003330950-5

Maybe, in the past, hugs were dangerous or led to abuse. Maybe, in the past, you were with a partner who rejected or refused you when you were having emotional needs. So, your anxiety is the message from inside of you telling you that something about your desire to ask for a hug is worrisome—new, different, and a little bit hard. That said, you can still ask for that hug! If you ask for that hug, you may still feel a little anxious or worried, yet you might get the hug and that would be information, or you might not get the hug, and that would be information too. No matter what you do in response to a feeling, you learn something, which you can use going forward into new situations.

- Sometimes, we fear that emotions are dangerous or a big problem. But what **is** the problem is all of the things that we do to avoid or get rid of feelings that seem overwhelming or frightening. Things like pushing feelings away, going numb, dissociating, self-injury, eating behaviours—these things are problematic. Having feelings, understanding them, and learning to know how to use the information they provide is **not** dangerous or bad!
- It is possible to:
  - be aware of our emotions and what they are trying to tell us,
  - express emotions in positive ways,
  - increase our ability to tolerate unpleasant emotions,
  - cope with stress effectively and in positive ways, and
  - behave effectively to match our values and reach our goals in stressful situations.

What do we mean by emotion regulation?

- Affects, feelings, or emotions are three words that mean the same thing: how we feel, emotionally, in response to the world around us, the world within us, and the relationships in which we engage.
- Feelings exist in many ways, and different people might feel very different things in response to the same experience.
- Often survivors of trauma have difficulty naming or understanding their feelings, tolerating feelings that may feel overwhelming and frightening, and then managing those feelings in ways that allow them to feel strong, capable, and safe.
- When survivors face these difficulties, couple relationships can feel very difficult. If you find it hard to name, tolerate, and manage your emotions when experiencing conflicts or difficulties with your partner, the emotions that you feel about these conflicts or difficulties may quickly overwhelm you and make it really hard for you to work through the problem in a healthy and constructive way. In fact, the problem becomes the feelings instead of the original conflict. This can leave conflicts and difficulties unresolved and partners feeling angry, hurt, resentful, and even frightened of bringing their concerns to their partner for fear that things will get worse or explode.
- This same problem happens in couple therapy. Often couples come to therapy to work through difficult conflicts that they have been unable to resolve on their own or they come to therapy to work on the negative interaction cycles or dyadic traumatic reenactments that we will explore further on in this section. When they come in to work on these issues and the survivor finds it difficult to name, tolerate, and then manage their feelings, the therapy quickly becomes focused on helping them feel emotionally safe again and the couple does not get the opportunity to really engage in the process of resolving these important conflicts.

It is absolutely possible to go from struggling and coping through turning away from your partner and to coping strategies that alienate you and make you feel even worse to...

Coping strategies to help you connect, grow, feel close and connected to yourself and to others.

JOURNAL REFLECTIONS HANDOUT: EMOTION REGULATION, TRAUMA, AND COUPLES

What are your personal experiences with feeling, naming, and managing emotions?

_____

_____

_____

_____

_____

_____

_____

How do you deal with feelings that are strong and threaten to overwhelm you?

_____

_____

_____

_____

_____

_____

How do you, as a couple, work together to support each other in emotion regulation?

_____

_____

_____

_____

_____

_____

How have you, as a couple, struggled with the impacts of difficulties with emotion regulation on your ability to work together and support one another?

_____

_____

_____

_____

_____

_____

_____

Primary and Secondary Emotions

A psychoeducational topic that was not in the original DCTCT treatment manual was *Primary and Secondary Emotions*. I am adding this section because we have found that once we dive deeper into the therapeutic work, this concept is really helpful for understanding our emotions, our emotional responses, our trauma triggers, and why, sometimes, the way we react to a situation or to our partner doesn't quite fit with what we really feel, deep down.

The simplest way of understanding the difference between a primary and a secondary emotion is that primary emotions are primary: they are the first emotion, the closest to the raw emotional response that is coming up for us. Secondary emotions are just that: they come second. Secondary emotions are the emotions that we may, totally unconsciously and automatically, thrust into the space that a primary emotion might occupy. We do this for many reasons, but the most common reason is that we just can't tolerate the primary emotion; perhaps it is too raw, too painful, too vulnerable, too frightening. So the secondary emotion comes jogging in and takes its place—less raw, less painful, less vulnerable, less frightening, but also farther away from connection.

Since the primary emotions are closer to the real experience you are having, they may feel more vulnerable, but they also draw your partner in closer. Imagine the difference between seeing your partner crying and seeing your partner raging: one tends to draw you closer, the other tends to push you away. In short, when we feel safe and connected enough it can be possible for us to experience our primary emotions, and these draw our partners closer to us to provide support and comfort. If we aren't feeling safe and connected enough, or an emotional response to a trauma memory or something that reminds us of being small and vulnerable is just too much, we engage our secondary emotions. This can push our partners away, leaving us feeling just as small, vulnerable, and alone as we might have been when we were small and being hurt.

Shame and anger can be **either** primary or secondary emotions, depending on the circumstances. Shame is very much a part of our evolution as a way of helping us know what is and isn't okay in our communities. Shame is a feeling that helps us know that we are outside of the norms of our communities, and it helps us know that we need to change some aspect of our behaviour to return to the fold of our social connections. This description fits when shame is a primary emotion. However, shame can also be a secondary emotion: it can be a reaction to feelings of hurt, sadness, guilt, and anger, among others. When

DOI: 10.4324/9781003330950-6

shame takes on the role of a secondary emotion, for trauma survivors, it can shut us down and make it impossible to stay connected to the outside of us, and to those around us. We can become so mired in shame that we are unable to see anything beyond our desire to disappear.

Anger is very similar. Anger is important for survival; you need to be able to feel anger if someone is threatening you or there is some harm that might come your way or to someone you care about. Anger helps us with that fight response that can be so important in protecting us. However, when we experience trauma, especially if we are in any kind of danger that would be made worse if we were to fight—like a child with a violent parent, where making themselves very small and invisible will help them survive and where fighting back might actually result in their death—anger as a primary emotion is often shut off and "squished" down. As a secondary emotion, anger can be a comforting antidote to feelings of grief, shame, hurt, and vulnerability but, like all secondary emotions, it can also alienate us from the very people we long to be close to.

Primary and Secondary Emotions

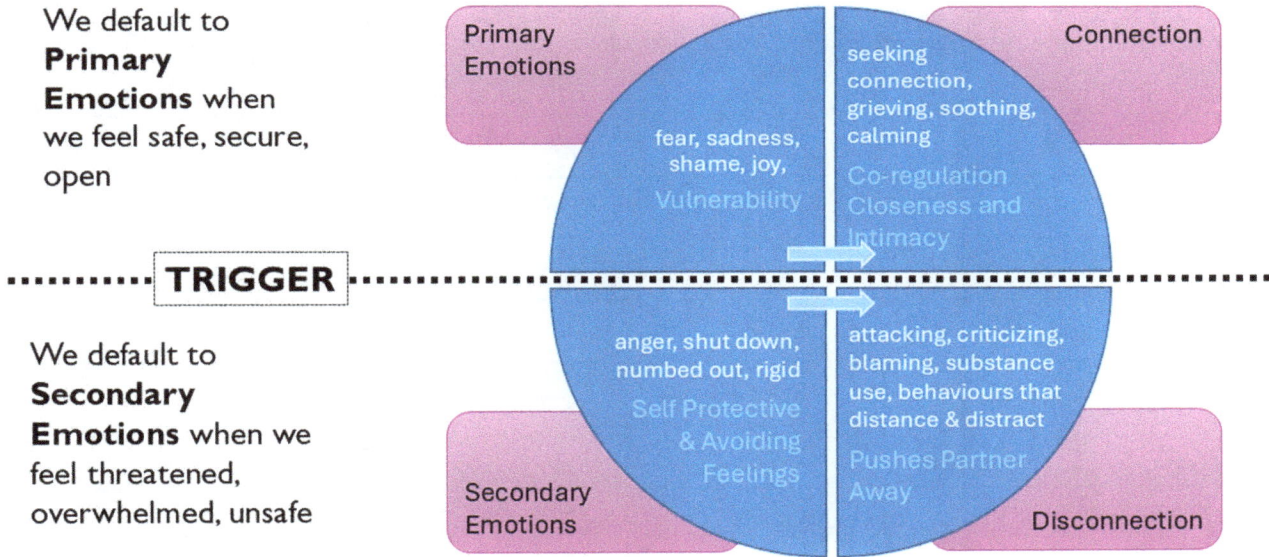

We default to **Primary Emotions** when we feel safe, secure, open

TRIGGER

We default to **Secondary Emotions** when we feel threatened, overwhelmed, unsafe

Primary Emotions

fear, sadness, shame, joy, Vulnerability

Connection

seeking connection, grieving, soothing, calming
Co-regulation Closeness and Intimacy

anger, shut down, numbed out, rigid
Self Protective & Avoiding Feelings

attacking, criticizing, blaming, substance use, behaviours that distance & distract
Pushes Partner Away

Secondary Emotions

Disconnection

JOURNAL REFLECTIONS HANDOUT: PRIMARY AND SECONDARY EMOTIONS

Can you think of a situation where you were aware that your feelings were maybe scary or too painful or too risky, and so, something else came out instead? Like a moment of feeling really hurt by your partner but, being in a public place or not being sure how your partner would respond to your hurt, what came out instead was anger that looked like sarcasm and insulting them?

_____

_____

_____

_____

_____

_____

Can you think of emotions that you find really difficult to tolerate and others that you find okay?

_____

_____

_____

_____

_____

_____

_____

_____

Shame

One of the most common emotions experienced by trauma survivors is shame. As survivors of trauma, especially childhood trauma, we often have difficulty feeling, naming, tolerating, and regulating our emotions. Shame, however, is the one emotion that can often be felt and named. In fact, it can obliterate all of the others. In my research and clinical practice, I've seen that most survivors have one emotion that is their default, the one emotion that comes rushing in over and above all others.

In some ways, shame is protective, it "smushes" everything else away, rendering all of the complexity and confusion of emotions that are triggered by how our lives and relationships continue to pull us back into the shame built into our bones by experiences that should never have happened. For most survivors, that emotion is shame. In this context,

DOI: 10.4324/9781003330950-7

shame is acting as a secondary emotion, protecting us from deeper feelings that might make it very difficult for us to cope and feel safe in our own bodies and relationships.

In the illustration on page 29 our blobby has come into the living room from doing meal preparation for the upcoming week and is curious about why their partner didn't hold up their end of the bargain and fold the laundry. Instead of being able to say—"well, I was just so exhausted I couldn't manage it" or, "one of the kids woke up and was feeling sick so I just didn't get to it"—the shame woke up and pulled them into the shame hole and they just dissolved into a puddle of shame. Not only were they not able to respond to their partner's legitimate question but they weren't able to ask for support or take responsibility for acknowledging that their partner had done their part of the workload division agreement, and that they had not. Shame keeps us from being able to seek support and from being able to take responsibility for the places where maybe we aren't holding up our end of the bargain.

HANDOUT: SHAME

What is shame, and how is it connected to trauma?

- Shame is an emotion that involves negative beliefs about yourself that can be pervasive and destructive to your sense of self. These feelings are strongly associated with experiences of childhood trauma.
- Shame is an emotion that can feel like it defines who you are as damaged, bad, helpless, and a failure. Shame is different from guilt. Guilt is a feeling of **doing** something bad. Shame is a feeling of **being** bad.
- Shame can be a response to secrecy, such as secrecy about sexual abuse or trauma and can lead to feelings of disconnection, detachment, and distress in relationships.
- Shame is a common response to trauma because it is sometimes easier to believe that there is something wrong with you than to believe that your abuser, often a parent or loved one, could hurt you for no reason.
- When childhood trauma includes sexual abuse, when abuse happens at earlier ages, or when a survivor believes that they were at fault for the abuse or even enjoyed aspects of the abuse, shame can be far worse and very painful.
- When boys are sexually abused, they can come to feel that they have failed as "men", failed to protect themselves and be strong, as men should be. This can lead to high levels of shame as sexual abuse of boys is still something that people think does not happen or, even that a boy is "lucky" to be abused by an older person who "initiates" them.

How might shame impact you?

- Shame can cause you to believe that you do not deserve to be in a happy, healthy relationship or that you are at fault when things go wrong in your life.
- Shame can cause you to feel that you are unable to take action in your life and relationships to make them better.
- Shame can cause you to feel so terrible about yourself that you hurt yourself through eating, drinking, drugs, sexual behaviours that feel shameful, or self-injury in the hopes that these things will soothe you or help you feel better. It is more common for female trauma survivors to respond to

feelings of shame by "internalizing" those feelings and turning their shame inwards through hurting themselves.

- For some people, when they feel ashamed, like thinking they are bad and have done something that makes them feel even worse, they can react by becoming aggressive, angry, or even violent. It is more common for male trauma survivors to "externalize", or react in these ways, and for them to find it unbearable to instead share how bad and vulnerable they feel, with their partners.
- Shame can cause you to feel the need to keep parts of yourself separate from other people, including important parts of your history of trauma and your intimate self that exists in your couple relationship.
- Shame keeps people from fully engaging in life and relationships.

Shame and LGBTQ+ and BIPOC survivors

- Growing up in a society that shames, discriminates and oppresses LGBTQ+ & BIPOC persons can lead to *internalized shame, self-hatred, and internalized racism/homophobia/transphobia.*
- Society sends us the clear message—being LGBTQ+/BIPOC/QTBIPOC can be dangerous and result in marginalization, oppression and, even, violence. There is also a message that our differences—aspects of *our very identity*—are a source of "badness".
- All of these things are *outside of ourselves* and yet, we can end up internalizing shame.

How can shame impact relationships?

- Shame can make people feel that they are unlovable and damaged, and this can lead them to believe that they do not deserve to be in a healthy, loving relationship or that they do not have the right to stand up for themselves in their relationships.
- Shame may lead people to avoid disclosing their traumatic experiences, which can keep you feeling separated and alienated from your partner.
- Shame can lead to people keeping other kinds of secrets, secrets about their sexuality, their feelings of hurt and pain, or secrets about things that need to be discussed and resolved for the relationship to be healthy.
- Shame can cause you to believe that you deserve to be in relationships where you might be hurt or treated poorly, and so shame can lead people to stay in relationships where it might be safer or healthier to separate.
- When someone feels strong feelings of shame it can make it very difficult for them to empathize with their partner, especially if their partner is upset about something that they themselves have done. It can cause them to be unable to hear their partner's concerns and to respond without being overwhelmed.
- When someone feels strong feelings of shame, this can cause them to protect themselves from the pain and vulnerability of these feelings. How they protect themselves might not be something that is healthy for them or their relationship.

Shame relates to the issues discussed above, such as self-injury or addictions that the trauma survivor might hide from their partner, or even the survivor becoming aggressive or violent towards their partner.

JOURNAL REFLECTIONS HANDOUT: SHAME AND YOUR RELATIONSHIP

How have you been aware of the impacts of shame on how you feel about yourself? How often do you feel shame, and what triggers cause you to feel shame?

_____

_____

_____

_____

_____

_____

Was shame used, in your childhood, as a way of "squishing" you down? Was it a part of your traumatic experiences in terms of how an abuser might have turned the responsibility of the trauma onto you?

_____

_____

_____

_____

_____

_____

_____

Where does shame come into play in your relationship?

_____

_____

_____

_____

_____

_____

_____

How do you cope or respond to feelings of shame? How does shame affect your ability to be close and sharing in your relationship?

_____

_____

_____

_____

_____

_____

_____

Do either you or your partner respond with shame to the needs or distress of each other? If so, what does that look like? If so, how does that impact resolution of the problem, need, or distress?

_____

_____

_____

_____

_____

_____

_____

Mentalizing

Mentalizing is a concept that is really helpful, once you feel you've figured it out. Through our clinical research we have seen that it can be a challenging concept to "get". In our DCTCT couple groups we introduce mentalizing and discuss it for a few weeks and, gradually, I can see the light go on inside of folks. They get very excited because, seemingly all of a sudden, something that felt so challenging to understand makes so much sense. However, this handout from the DCTCT treatment manual is pretty dense.

One of my defaults is to use too many words, and my students often catch this before things get too far, but I wrote this when I was first developing the treatment manual. We've found that it's really in the exercises and reflections that folks find their way into understanding mentalizing. Read through it a few times and see if it makes sense to you.

I've added some examples after the handout to put some flesh onto the bones, so to speak. If it doesn't make sense at first, that's okay, just do the journal reflections and sit with it. Some concepts require practice and reflection before they find their way into our bodies as well-understood resources for our healing.

HANDOUT: MENTALIZING

What is mentalizing?

- Mentalizing is an imaginative mental activity that helps us perceive and understand others and ourselves. Through mentalizing, we can make sense of others and ourselves by understanding both clearly expressed and more subtle signals about their emotional states and mental processes.
- When you learn how to mentalize well, you can then think about, reflect on, hold, and explore emotions, thoughts, and mental states. Strong mentalizing capacities are fundamental to a person's ability to have positive relationships and manage in social environments.
- Strong mentalizing can be seen when someone is easily able to explore their own mental states and has interest in the mental states of others. These individuals understand how mental states change and can integrate thoughts and emotional aspects of themselves and others. They have the ability to regulate their own and other's distress and to be playful and solve problems through give and take.
- People who can mentalize well are able to take responsibility and acknowledge their own behaviour. They are curious about other people's perspectives and are comfortable with uncertainty. As you might imagine, these capacities are essential for a healthy and happy couple relationship.

DOI: 10.4324/9781003330950-8

- Poor mentalizing can be seen when someone is unable to reflect on their own thoughts and feelings and makes automatic assumptions about others that may not be accurate. These people find it very difficult to tolerate and regulate their own or others' distress, and they tend to be rather rigid and certain about what they and others might be thinking, feeling, and understanding, often without any exploration or discussion.

How does trauma impact mentalizing?

Studies suggest that those who have experienced abuse generally have lower mentalizing capacities. This relationship goes two ways:

- First, trauma can make it very difficult for a child to develop the capacity to mentalize well. For instance, a traumatized or dissociated caregiver sends the message to the child that their internal world is bad or dangerous, through their lack of understanding of their own distressed state and that of the child. This leaves the child feeling disoriented and confused. Also, when traumas occur, a child should be able to turn to their caregiver for soothing, support, and comfort. What then does a child do when the caregiver is the person who inflicts the trauma? Getting closer to the caregiver might lead to more abuse, more distress, and more need.
- Second, it can also be dangerous for an abused child to mentalize. Not only can it be more dangerous to turn to an abusing caregiver in terms of the potential for more abuse, but mentalizing can also be dangerous for the developing mind of the abused child. Imagine being able to think about what is going on in the mind of the abuser, someone who is intentionally hurting a child physically, sexually, or emotionally. This could be incredibly terrifying and emotionally dangerous for a child. The best defense against this is to avoid thinking about the mind of the abuser altogether. However, this then means that the child never develops these essential skills to build and maintain relationships.

How is mentalizing relevant to couple therapy?

- Mentalizing is an essential capacity for being able to get into and then nurture a healthy romantic relationship. Without being able to reflect upon and tolerate your own thoughts, feelings, and behaviours and those of your partner, a couple relationship would be very difficult. Mentalizing makes it possible to acknowledge and take responsibility for ourselves in relationships, to have empathy and compassion for each other, to be vulnerable and open, and to have safe and clear boundaries with your partner.
- When people experience trauma in childhood, their mentalizing capacities can either not develop or be damaged. This means that it can be hard for a trauma survivor to think about and understand their own feelings, thoughts, and behaviours as well as those of their partner. If you combine this with difficulties in emotion regulation, it can be very difficult to talk about or navigate difficult or painful issues. At the beginning of a relationship, when things are fresh and there has not been an accumulation of painful hurts or conflicts, things may be somewhat manageable, but as relationships move along, it is inevitable that conflicts will arise, one partner will hurt the other's feelings, and difficult life events will crop up that require the use of these mentalizing and emotion regulation skills.
- Couples that have experienced trauma may find it very difficult to do some of the things that couples need to do to repair hurts and conflicts and just to function day by day. These include being able to help each other feel better and safe with each other, take responsibility for how they impact and affect each other, tolerate that they may not know everything about their partner and their feelings, be curious and playful with and about one another, avoid becoming defensive when important discussions arise, correct and repair misunderstandings, not get stuck when misunderstandings arise, trust one another, and be responsive to one another.

Can mentalizing capacities be developed in adulthood?

In adulthood, if one has not learned how to mentalize or one's capacity to mentalize was damaged by trauma, it is important to work actively to develop these capacities. Practice is the most important approach to learning these skills.

With your partner, you can practise these skills in everyday normal situations:

- You can ask questions of your partner about their thoughts, feelings, and behaviours.
- You can take a moment to share your assumptions about what is happening in that moment, listen actively, and work on changing your assumptions in response to what your partner tells you.
- You can be curious about what is happening in your own and your partner's mind in response to situations that might have gotten you into conflict in the past, by slowing down, listening, not making assumptions, taking a moment to step away and calm down, coming back together and reflecting on what has just happened, and trying to understand and empathize with your partner even when it is painful or difficult to do so.

In essence, then, when we mentalize well we can be curious, open-minded, interested, and aware that we can't always know what's going on inside someone else, even for our partner. When we struggle to mentalize well, we can shut down, make a lot of assumptions, and stick to them like glue. We find it hard to be open and curious about what's going on with our partner, shutting down any parts of ourselves that might be able to figure it out.

Trauma can make it so hard to stay open and curious because we learned, early on, that to be curious about the experiences of others could be dangerous. Imagine being curious about the thoughts, feelings, sensations, and impulses of someone who has been sexually abusing you; it would crush your soul. So it's better to just shut that all out and then, when we find ourselves in relationships with people who aren't going to intentionally hurt us, we don't know where to start with opening up our curiosity and openness.

In the following chart, take a look at the characteristics of mentalizing and see if you can notice where you do pretty well and where you might struggle.

When mentalizing well...	When mentalizing is more challenging...
I can easily access & explore my inner world	I'm not sure what I am feeling, thinking, wanting, or needing
I'm curious & interested in other people's inner worlds	I jump to conclusions or make assumptions about others
I can tolerate & regulate distress	I can't tolerate my distress &/or other people's distress
I can be playful & problem solve through give & take	I become stuck & rigid when problems/conflicts arise
I can hold my perspective & my partner's at the same time	When my partner & I disagree, it feels like only one of us can be right
I am comfortable with uncertainty	Uncertainty feels intolerable & I need to know *now*

Examples of Mentalizing

Mentalizing Well

A simple example of strong mentalizing could be when your partner is very upset about something—they are storming around the house and you are trying to connect with them, but they are *not* engaging with your attempts. In this moment, as you are mentalizing well, you are curious about what is going on with your partner, you aren't making assumptions, and you certainly aren't leaping to the conclusion that your partner is mad at you. In this moment of strong mentalizing you are approaching them, letting them know that you are curious about what is going on: you can see that something is upsetting them, but it's also okay if they aren't ready to let you in. You can tolerate not knowing, you can be curious about what is going on inside your partner that might help you understand what is happening on the outside of your partner. You can also tolerate waiting until they are ready to share with you.

Eventually, your partner shares with you that someone at their workplace said something really hurtful to them. They explain that this was someone in a position of authority, so they felt that they had to button up and not express their hurt or anger. Now they are feeling angry about feeling vulnerable and about feeling like they couldn't respond in a way that protected themselves from this hurtful thing.

Mentalizing Struggles

If we imagine how this situation would look if you, as the partner, were struggling to mentalize, we would see a very different picture. For the first instance, if you saw how upset your partner was, storming around, you might easily make assumptions about what is happening inside of them and, very likely, you would assume that it was *you* that they were upset with. You might start making connections to things that happened in the past—to things inside of you that are upsetting you and that you imagine your partner is also upset by. In this scenario, you may lose your capacity to hold any curiosity or empathy for your struggling partner.

Along with your shut down of curiosity, you may also find that your ability to regulate your emotions goes out the window, and you start to panic about what's going on. As you panic, you approach your partner with more and more intensity. Since they are already activated and upset, perhaps their mentalizing capacities have also shut down, they tell you that they can't talk about it—with some intensity. Not only does this end up confirming that your partner is upset with you, but it confirms to your partner that they have to retreat from you, perhaps both physically and emotionally. You may also lose your curiosity and empathy, which might hinder your ability to be open to hearing what's really going on with your partner. At the same time, your partner may shut you out because they are feeling pressured and pushed.

Takeaways

You can see that in the strong mentalizing example the partner is upset but you are curious and open, and you can tolerate not knowing. When your partner is able to regulate themselves enough, they can share their difficulty with you, and then you both talk about the situation to help your partner settle and work on a solution, recognizing how they are feeling and how they might address the problem.

In the not-so-good mentalizing example your partner is upset, and you fall into making assumptions that are backed up by all sorts of things inside of you, rather than staying curious and open to what's actually happening with your partner. In your inability to tolerate not knowing, you pursue, which shuts down your partner even more. In the end, your partner won't share with you and you are left in a distressed state that only confirms your assumptions that your partner is upset with you—even though their upset had nothing to do with you.

JOURNAL REFLECTIONS HANDOUT: MENTALIZING

What comes to mind when you think about mentalizing and *your own experiences* of yourself?

_____

_____

_____

_____

_____

_____

Where do you see yourself in the "mentalizing well" category and the "mentalizing poorly" category in the *characteristics of mentalizing*?

_____

_____

_____

_____

_____

_____

_____

Do you notice moments where your personal *capacity to mentalize* flies out the window? What are those moments, and triggers?

_____

_____

_____

_____

_____

_____

_____

How do you, as a couple, notice being more or less able to mentalize one another? What are your strengths? What are your challenges?

_____

_____

_____

_____

_____

_____

_____

How have you, as a couple, struggled with the *impacts of difficulties with mentalizing* on your ability to work together as a couple and support one another?

_____

_____

_____

_____

_____

_____

_____

Trauma and Attachment

You've probably heard about attachment theory in therapy or in your own research on understanding how trauma may have impacted your *self* and your relationships. Attachment theory is important in helping us understand how we approach relationships, what we expect, what we believe, how we move forward or back away, which are all aspects of our selves that can be influenced by attachment. The following section gives a primer on attachment theory, and we will discuss it in depth in Stage Three.

HANDOUT: TRAUMA AND ATTACHMENT

What do we mean by attachment?

The term "attachment" relates to the relationships we have with the significant others in our lives. In particular, we are referring to the relationship between an infant and their primary caregiver and the relationship between romantic partners.

There are different ways of being attached:

- The majority of people (70%) have mostly positive experiences of closeness with their primary caregivers in infancy and childhood and these people, called **securely attached**, come to believe that people would be there for them in their distress and that they, themselves, were worthy of care and comfort from others.
- A smaller percentage of people experience relationships with their primary caregivers that cause them to feel **insecure attachment**. People with inconsistent and unresponsive experiences with caregivers often have Internal Working Models that cause them to be unsure about whether they, themselves, are worthy of consistent care to be unsure about whether people will be there for them.
- There are three different ways to be insecurely attached, based on different combinations of how we feel about ourselves and others.
- Research with couples has demonstrated that attachment security/insecurity is quite consistent from childhood to adulthood. This research also indicates that the needs for closeness, safety, and a "secure base" are lifelong needs. This tells us that if someone has a secure attachment in childhood, they will likely have a secure attachment also with their romantic partner.

DOI: 10.4324/9781003330950-9

How does childhood trauma impact attachment?

- Childhood trauma may have a significant impact on attachment. The earlier in your life the trauma happens and the closer the relationship with your abuser, the more significant the impact of the trauma is on your attachment security.
- Most childhood trauma survivors do experience some insecurity in their attachment relationships.
- For those who have experienced sexual abuse, attachment insecurity can be even more complicated. For instance, while you may long for connection and closeness with others, that very same closeness and connection may feel dangerous. This can lead to difficulties with maintaining close relationships and a tendency to jump into relationships quickly, becoming overwhelmed and frightened, and then running away.

While about 70% of people are securely attached, most childhood trauma survivors fall into one of the insecure categories of attachment. But how can you be securely attached when your world was scary, if your caregivers were dangerous, and if you didn't know where to turn when things were falling apart? The four attachment styles can be understood as combinations of how we feel about ourselves and what we expect from and believe about others.

Look at the Four Styles of Attachment chart to see those two dimensions. *Low or High Avoidance* means: do I avoid others because I don't trust that they will be there for me or safe? Or do I think others are pretty okay, pretty safe, not dangerous? *Low or High Anxiety* means: am I afraid that I'm not good enough, not loveable enough, for people to care for me, protect me, or love me? Or do I think that I'm not so bad, pretty loveable, worthy of being cared for? It's the combinations of these that, put together, make our attachment style.

Four Styles of Attachment

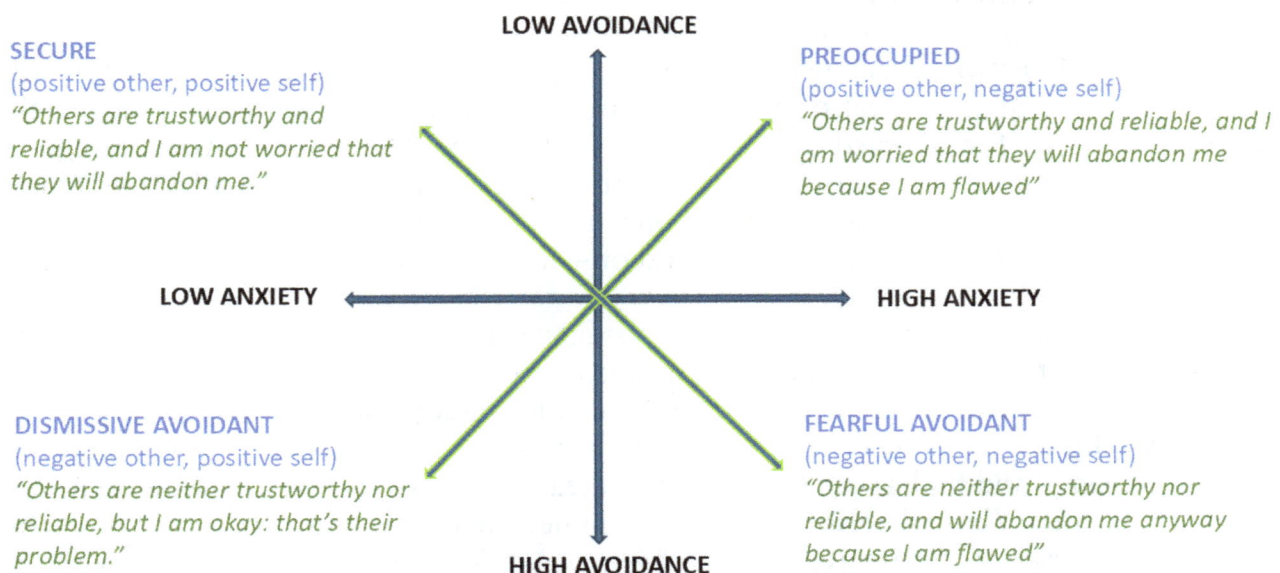

LOW AVOIDANCE

SECURE
(positive other, positive self)
"Others are trustworthy and reliable, and I am not worried that they will abandon me."

PREOCCUPIED
(positive other, negative self)
"Others are trustworthy and reliable, and I am worried that they will abandon me because I am flawed"

LOW ANXIETY ←→ **HIGH ANXIETY**

DISMISSIVE AVOIDANT
(negative other, positive self)
"Others are neither trustworthy nor reliable, but I am okay: that's their problem."

FEARFUL AVOIDANT
(negative other, negative self)
"Others are neither trustworthy nor reliable, and will abandon me anyway because I am flawed"

HIGH AVOIDANCE

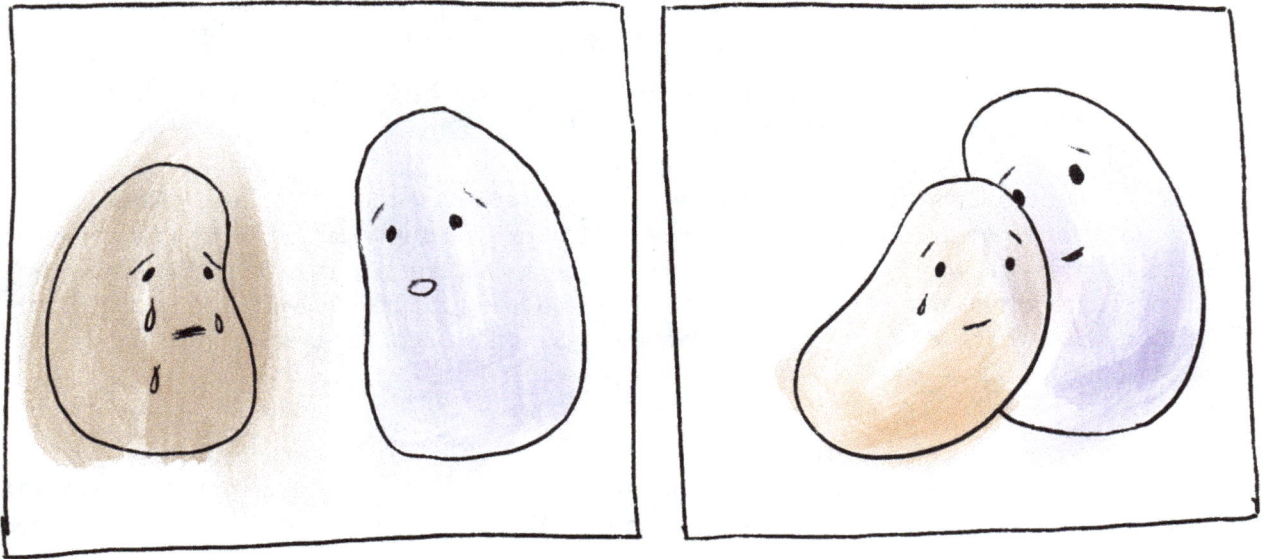

SECURE ATTACHMENT

The ***Preoccupied*** attachment style brings together a model of self that is negative—that I am not worthy of care, and a model of others that is positive—that others are worth connecting with and are valuable. Persons who experience their attachment relationships from this perspective are often relentlessly pursuing a partner while also finding it impossible to believe that a partner might ever want them or want to be with them.

The ***Avoidant*** attachment style is pretty much the polar opposite of the Preoccupied. The person who experiences their attachment relationships from an avoidant stance sees themselves as worthy and others as dangerous and not worth connecting with. Of course, part of the trick here is that this is also not necessarily true. For many trauma survivors, assuming an avoidant stance is a way of protecting themselves from further hurt and pain—*I'm just fine, it's people who are the problem!*

The ***Fearful Avoidant*** attachment style is the style most associated with a history of trauma. This particular orientation to connection with others is, in essence, a flipping back and forth between Preoccupied and Avoidant. I call it the "Approach—Avoid Tango". Survivors can be found to pursue connection with a partner who they feel is all of the things that they are not (Preoccupied) and then, once they have gotten up close and personal, they run away (Avoidant). This can go on and on—hence the tango—until the prospective partner walks away.

And, of course, partners come with our own baggage and attachment histories and styles, so we often find the lock to our key. For instance, the Preoccupied survivor can reliably find themselves an Avoidant partner and vice versa. It's handy and oh so stressful!

While attachment styles tend to be consistent across our lives, that does not mean that we cannot change and find a way to experience greater security and safety in our relationships with partners. ***Earned Security*** is our goal in healing ourselves and our relationships. While trauma survivors often have Internal Working Models (IWM) that tell us that we can *expect people will not be there* for us when we need them and tell us that *we are not worthy* of love and care there is something called Earned Security. Over time, with *consistency*, *empathy*, *responsiveness*, *co-regulation*, trauma survivors can develop "earned security" with a partner. Over time we can learn to override those IWMs. We may still default to our baseline attachment style when we are under stress, but we can also gradually become more secure if we are able to hold onto new experiences of consistency and reliability in new relationships—learning to pay attention to the cues that are not what we expect.

EARNED SECURE ATTACHMENT

JOURNAL REFLECTIONS HANDOUT: ATTACHMENT AND TRAUMA

Where do you see yourself in these descriptions? If you had to place yourself in one of the categories, which one would you choose?

_____

_____

_____

_____

_____

_____

_____

Why would you choose that category? What about how you feel about your *self* do you feel fits with that category?

_____

_____

_____

_____

_____

_____

_____

What about how you feel about and expect from *others* do you feel fits with that category?

_____

_____

_____

_____

_____

_____

_____

Do you tend to be anxious about whether others will let you down or abandon you?

_____

_____

_____

_____

_____

_____

_____

Do you tend to avoid closeness with others and fear that they will hurt you if you let yourself get close?

_____

_____

_____

_____

_____

_____

How do you understand the origins of these feelings about your *self* and *others*?

_____

_____

_____

_____

_____

_____

_____

How has this affected your relationships?

_____

_____

_____

_____

_____

_____

_____

Thinking about some developmental experiences that might influence how you grew into who you are now and how you form attachments:

Who were the people you felt close to, as a child?

_____

_____

_____

_____

_____

_____

Who were your role models growing up, and why?

_____

_____

_____

_____

_____

_____

_____

Who did you go to when you were upset as a child? What did you do when you were upset as a child?

_____

_____

_____

_____

_____

_____

_____

What is your earliest memory of being taken care of or comforted? Who were the people you felt comfortable being held or hugged by? What was it like to be sick in your family?

_____

_____

_____

_____

_____

_____

_____

Negative Cycles and Dyadic Traumatic Reenactment (DTR)

All couples have a negative cycle—it's how we get caught up in a conflict and we feel like we are having the same fight that we've had 500 times before. This time it's about who took out the garbage but the last time it was about spending too much on the groceries.

Negative cycles feel familiar, stuck, and sometimes just stupid, because when you look at it you think—um—why did we get so upset about that? Then, add trauma to the mix and it's like putting negative cycles on steroids—they just expand and grow because not only do you have the thing you are upset about, you have all of the emotional needs, attachment needs, and real upset. Much of the time, what is happening in the present conflict is also triggering some old stuff, from trauma times.

It's like having a triple espresso that makes you jump inside your skin and keeps you awake for three days instead of just that one nice single espresso that keeps you focused at work.

HANDOUT: NEGATIVE CYCLES AND DYADIC TRAUMATIC REENACTMENT

What do we mean by a negative cycle?

- Many couples who come to couple therapy say that they have the same argument over and over again and that they just cannot escape the pattern that they get stuck in no matter how hard they try.
- In couple relationships, especially when there is a history of childhood trauma, attempts to get our attachment needs and longings met by our partners sometimes result in disappointment, hurt feelings, and discouragement. When partners are feeling angry, discouraged, and hurt, they can often turn to "secondary emotions" as a way of protecting themselves from further hurt. For example, instead of showing our partner how hurt and sad we feel, we may lash out in anger. In response, our partner may simply withdraw from our angry or critical approach, and these types of interactions lead the couple into a repetitive cycle of hide-and-seek, where one partner is longing for connection and the other is running. In couples where there is a history of trauma, shame and fear about connection can be a big factor in this negative interaction cycle.
- Often, how one partner responds to a distressing interaction can result in an almost opposite response from their partner, such as: *I seek you out and you move away from me.* Frequently, the response is exactly the opposite to what we feel we need in that moment and, often, we end up feeling more hurt and alone than we did before the interaction.

DOI: 10.4324/9781003330950-10

What do we mean by a Dyadic Traumatic Reenactment (DTR)?

- Childhood trauma frequently occurs in the context of relationships with people who should have cared for and protected a child. The traumas often have a significant impact on the survivor's capacity to trust and feel safe in adult relationships.
- When we experience these kinds of traumas, our memories, feelings, expectations, and fears follow us into our important relationships. When looking at the patterns and cycles of couples where one or both partners have experienced childhood trauma, we see that the past has gotten stuck there and clings to the cycle that unfolds between them with a lot of force.
- In therapy, survivors can often identify and articulate what happens between them, understand it and sometimes even begin to stop it. However, when it comes to really getting to the bottom of it and changing it, many childhood trauma survivors get stuck at this point in therapy and keep repeating the patterns with increasing frustration: they keep sliding back into the chaos and pain of their early traumas as they are relived with each other.
- Part of the process of understanding the DTR is to externalize the trauma as a force that you and your partner are fighting together, a force that makes it very difficult to shift out of these negative cycles. It is very difficult to make the shift from insight and understanding to real change, when the thing we are trying to change is not something we are even aware of.
- For many couples, this powerful pull of unprocessed trauma happens because the trauma has not been "symbolized" or made conscious and put into words. Being able to think and know our traumas, not just the details, but the feelings and sensations of those deeply embedded experiences, allows someone to talk about their traumas as a part of their life story and to really "get" how these traumas have impacted their relationships. These unsymbolized traumas typically remain stubbornly stuck in their cycle. When traumatic emotions and memories or feelings continue to be unconscious and dissociated, they continue to be alive in the underworld of the couple's interactions. To help you with these trauma cycles, we have to work at a deeper level. We have to find ways to bring those stuck traumas into our minds and bodies so they can be talked about and explored. This can be a real challenge, because it involves paying attention to the ways in which we "find" the trauma being relived in our couple relationship; these can be hard and painful. However, your therapist will help you learn to pay attention to these parts of the cycle so you can start to really pull those stuck traumatic relivings out of your cycle and begin to build a new relationship where your interactions with your partner are not based on reliving traumas from the past.

Exercise: Identify the Negative Cycle

Take a look at the chart in Table 1.1 and fill in the answers to the prompts in the first column. This will help you understand more about your negative cycle. Some examples appear in the second column. Even starting to understand how these negative cycles get going and why can be a game changer for many couples. However, for trauma survivors, it's often the case that our understanding isn't enough on its own, to bring about change because of the DTR—the trauma that gets stuck into our negative cycles can make it really hard to see, feel, hear, and sense the difference between past and present. The exercise that follows the chart can help you start to understand how trauma is embedded in your negative cycle, your unique DTR.

Table 1.1 Exercise: Identify the Negative Cycle

When we get caught in the same argument we've had 3000000 times and we can't seem to get out:	
I feel...	Primary & Secondary Emotions
What I do then is...	E.g., pursuit: criticize, blame, demand, yell, say nasty things. E.g., withdraw: pull away, give up, shut down, go silent.
Even though I _____ what I really need is...	What is the attachment need? E.g., that you will help me feel safe, understood, etc.
When this happens my partner......	
When my partner does that, I feel....	
And then we both....	
When I react the way I do, I think my partner feels?	
Describe your negative cycle	**How do you and your partner trigger each other's feelings, thoughts, and behaviours?**

JOURNAL REFLECTIONS HANDOUT: IDENTIFY THE NEGATIVE CYCLE AND DTR

Through the exercise, can you identify a repeating argument or negative cycle in your relationship?

_____

_____

_____

_____

_____

_____

_____

How does it feel when you are pulled into your negative cycle?

_____

_____

_____

_____

_____

_____

_____

Can you identify aspects of your trauma that get triggered when this happens?

_____

_____

_____

_____

_____

_____

_____

What strategies have you tried to work on your negative cycle?

_____

_____

_____

_____

_____

_____

_____

What strategies have you tried to work on with regard to how trauma gets activated in your couple relationship and negative cycle?

_____

_____

_____

_____

_____

_____

_____

How well have these strategies worked for you and your partner? If well, what has been the most important thing you have done to find your way out of your negative cycle? If not so well, what do you feel like you've tried but it hasn't really helped?

_____

_____

_____

_____

_____

_____

_____

Sex and Sexuality After Trauma

Trauma comes in many forms, including sexual and non-sexual abuse in childhood, and other forms of interpersonal violence across the lifespan. Many people believe that it is only sexual trauma that leads to challenges with sex and sexuality. However, over the past decade we have been doing more and more research into how trauma impacts sex and sexuality and it is very clear that all kinds of traumas, at all ages and stages, can lead to struggles with sex and sexuality.

For survivors of non-sexual abuse, interpersonal traumas may lead to difficulties with trust, self-image, or identity, such that they do not feel that it is safe to be close to another person in a sexual or vulnerable way. For many trauma survivors, the embodied ways that trauma lingers and keeps us living the memories can make it really hard to let our guards down enough to allow sexual sensations through the protective layer of holding steady for survival. For others, traumas have alienated them from themselves and their bodies so much that they don't know themselves well enough to know who they might be attracted to or what they might enjoy, sexually.

Trauma lives in all parts of ourselves, our bodies, minds, and spirits—whatever language you might use for the part of ourselves that cannot be seen on an MRI or measured. In a way, trauma is the opposite of sexuality and sensuality—how can we feel sexual and sensual when our bodies are holding memories, feelings, arousal, and tensions from experiences that close us up and shut us down?

For survivors of sexual abuse, the consequences for adult sex and sexuality can be very complicated both directly and indirectly. These impacts might be different depending on the age when the abuse occurred, your sex or gender identity, or if the abuser was a same-sex or opposite-sex perpetrator.

And then, our bodies, for many of us, have become battlegrounds as we struggle our way through recovery and healing, striving to find ways to come to terms with how our bodies betrayed us, were used by others for their pleasure, were hurt and damaged in ways that can cause shame and deep memories of hurt, loss, and pain. For so many of us, our relationship with our bodies is so incredibly complicated and conflicted that the possibility of opening, joyfully, playfully, and curiously, into our sexuality can feel virtually impossible.

DOI: 10.4324/9781003330950-11

HANDOUT: SEX AND SEXUALITY AFTER TRAUMA

How might childhood trauma impact sex and sexuality in adults?

- Childhood trauma comes in many forms, including sexual and non-sexual abuse.
- For survivors of non-sexual abuse, childhood trauma may lead to difficulties with trust, self-image, or identity, such that they do not feel that it is safe to be close to another person or even to know themselves well enough to feel that they know who they might be attracted to or what they might enjoy, sexually.
- For survivors of sexual abuse, the consequences for adult sex and sexuality can be very complicated both directly and indirectly. These impacts might be different depending on the age when the abuse occurred, your sex or gender identity, or if the abuser was a same-sex or opposite-sex perpetrator.

How might sexual abuse impact an adult survivor?

- Childhood sexual abuse can make it hard for you to feel safe sexually and to feel like you can be fully open to your sexual feelings and desires.
- Childhood sexual abuse often happens before puberty, before the full development of your adult sexual body. Stimulating a body sexually, through force or through attempts to sexually arouse a child, can throw off the gradual and slow development of sexual responses and lead to problems with sexual pain, or difficulties with becoming aroused and having orgasms in adulthood.
- Childhood sexual abuse can cause some survivors to experience certain kinds of sexual activities or stimulation as triggering of flashbacks or nightmares.
- Some survivors find it hard to know what they do and do not find sexually pleasurable, and this can leave them feeling unsatisfied, disconnected from their arousal, as though they are just pleasing their partner without any pleasure for themselves and, even lead them to engage in sexual activities that end up feeling retraumatizing.
- Some survivors find that their sexual responses become "conditioned" to things connected to their abuse. That can often happen if the abuse itself was both arousing and painful or exciting and frightening. This can mean that survivors might be really turned on by things that, as an adult, now confuse, disgust, or frighten them. This can mean that they feel very turned on by things that are painful or involve harm to themselves or someone else. These kinds of conditioned sexual responses can be embarrassing, shameful, hurtful, or leave a survivor feeling alienated from themselves and their partner. To avoid these strong feelings, many survivors keep secrets to protect themselves and their partners.
- For some survivors, especially boys abused by men, this can mean that they are turned on sexually by adult men but identify as straight. This can cause them to feel anxious or confused about their sexual orientation.
- For some survivors, their gender identity and/or sexual orientation was a part of why they were targeted for sexual abuse by a perpetrator. Appearing vulnerable, different, even taking advantage of a child's need for care and support when families may have been rejecting of their gender identity or sexual orientation, can put many children at risk. Over and over, I have heard my patients talk about how they knew they had a "target" on their backs because they felt isolated, different, and unprotected.
- When one is targeted for sexual abuse due to an aspect of their identity it can make their growing into their gender identity and sexuality so much more complicated. For many, it then paints

a complexity on their coming out to themselves and the world that leads to years more of being closeted, more secrecy, more alienation from self and others, and so much more shame and so much less joy and pleasure in acknowledging and living fully in our bodies and relationships as queer and trans persons.

How can the sexual impacts of trauma affect relationships?

- Being triggered by certain sexual positions or kinds of stimulation can make feeling close and safe in your sexual relationship with your partner very difficult and can feel frustrating and painful.
- Being triggered by certain sexual positions or kinds of stimulation can leave your partner feeling as though they are hurting you or feeling like they are getting it wrong with you, especially if you can't talk about it.
- Having sexual pain can make it difficult to fully enjoy your sexual relationship with your partner.
- If the things that turn you on are things that you feel bad about, it can be hard to share these things with your partner, which may lead you to keep those parts of your sexual life a secret.

Trauma, the Body, and Sex

For so many trauma survivors, the aftermath of the struggle for survival lives in our bodies. It lives in our bodies as embedded memories of unknowable suffering. It lives in our bodies as expressions of boundaries that previously could not be voiced. For many of us, our bodies become representations of things that have happened to us and there is a disconnection and dissociation that emerges to help us survive all that is living in our bodies as memories, feelings, sensations, and impulses related to trauma. For trans and non/binary, racialized, indigenous, fat, otherly abled, and others whose bodies have also been a source of oppression, violence, or trauma, the complexity of finding our ways towards an affirming, loving, and gentle embodiment that allows for the healing of our sexual selves can be painful, arduous, and requires a lot of time and persistence.

Journal Reflections: Trauma, Sex, and Sexuality

If your sexual relationships are fraught with pain and conflict, these journaling reflections could be done on your own and shared with a partner later, if that feels safe and right. If you are in a couple relationship, go ahead and respond to the questions based on your current relationship.

However, if you are not in a relationship currently or, you feel that your reflections take you to another partner or partners, in another time in your life, that is also okay, just follow where your impulse takes you.

If you are able to share these reflections with your partner, great. If it doesn't feel possible at this time, that's also okay. Trust yourself to know what you can and cannot yet tolerate and what you and your partner are ready to process together.

Remember to take a deep breath and go slowly, take breaks if you start to feel overwhelmed or triggered, and even write about your responses and reactions as you are also responding to the questions.

DOI: 10.4324/9781003330950-12

JOURNAL REFLECTIONS HANDOUT: TRAUMA, SEX, AND SEXUALITY

How has your relationship been impacted by any sexual impacts of your trauma?

_____

_____

_____

_____

_____

_____

_____

What are the feelings, activities or sexual acts, touches, tastes, sensations, that might trigger you into a traumatized state of reliving? Can you make a list and connect a sensation or activity with a memory or memories?

_____

_____

_____

_____

_____

_____

_____

What kinds of flashbacks would you say are more common for you in sexual situations—body, mind, emotions, sensations?

_____

_____

_____

_____

_____

_____

_____

How would it feel to share and discuss these with your partner?

_____

_____

_____

_____

_____

_____

How do you cope with feelings of fear or avoidance in your sexual relationship?

_____

_____

_____

_____

_____

_____

_____

Are there aspects of your identity—sexual orientation, gender identity, among others, that are stuck together with your experiences of trauma? How might these impact your sexual life now, in adult relationships?

_____

_____

_____

_____

_____

_____

_____

Have you been able to talk together about what turns you on and what you would like more of or less of?

_____

_____

_____

_____

_____

_____

Do you have sexual pain and, if so, what resources have you been able to tap into to help you manage and treat this pain?

_____

_____

_____

_____

_____

_____

Stage Two

Building Capacity

When we are in distress and feeling overwhelmed with the impacts of our own traumas, the ways in which trauma is living our relationship, we want to move fast and fierce to anyplace other than where we are. Of course, moving forward and finding new ways of being and living in your relationship and your self is absolutely where we are heading but, as they say, slow but steady wins the race.

This next section focuses on building the skills and capacities that you will need to navigate the way forward. I know it can feel frustrating to be putting all this time, energy, and effort into learning and building capacities when all we really want is to feel safe, close, and connected to our partner. However, if you try to start climbing the ladder on the tenth rung, chances are good, it's going to be really challenging. The first section created a firm footing for the ladder and got you up the first few steps. Now we need to keep climbing, rung by rung, to get to the destination as we build some of the skills and capacities of which our traumatizing experiences deprived us.

These skills and capacities, including Emotion Regulation and Mentalizing, are the flesh on the bones of our newfound cognitive understanding of what trauma is all about and how it infiltrates our relationships. Even if you are keen to hop over to the next section and get going on processing traumas and building a stronger attachment, I would really encourage you to linger here for a while and put in the training required to be prepared for the race. Even I, who can't run faster than Molly the pig trying to get away with an apple in her mouth, can tell you, putting in the training before the race is going to pay off in the long run.

All the handouts in the book are available for download at www.routledge.com/9781032362465.

DOI: 10.4324/9781003330950-13

Skills Building in Emotion Regulation

In this section of the workbook, we are going to learn, reflect, and experiment with trying some new strategies to build emotion regulation capacities from scratch.

In the first section of the workbook, I introduced the idea of *Emotion Regulation* as something that can be significantly impacted by experiences of trauma, especially in childhood. Being unable to regulate our emotions when we are feeling big feelings, ones that we believe to be "good" or "bad", can make it difficult to function in all areas of our lives, especially in our relationships.

If we think about emotion regulation as something that develops in relationships it can help us understand how vital a capacity it is for us to embody in our relationships. When our caregivers help us with our emotions, when we are small and helpless, they show us from the "outside" how to manage the feelings that come with day-to-day life. In infancy these feelings can be about physical things like being hungry, tired, wet, or in pain. These feelings can also be about our emotional states in response to being alone, afraid, or angry, and all of the complicated ways that our bodies and vulnerable selves can be confusing and frightening.

Having a caregiver respond by being curious and interested in our physical or emotional state, and then make efforts to understand and *do* things to help, shows us that our feelings can be tolerated, understood, and regulated. This happens from the "outside", in essence, watching someone else do the regulating of us, for us. As we grow, gradually we become able to do the regulating from the "inside". We slowly internalize our caregivers' response and bring it "inside" so that we learn to do the regulating of ourselves, for ourselves.

When that process doesn't unfold, due to traumas, caregiver mental health difficulties, and other obstacles to caregiver attunement, we can grow into the complexities, stresses, and relational challenges of adulthood without developing the capacity for regulating with our close ones (co-regulation) or for ourselves (self-regulation).

In essence, we learn how to regulate our emotions through the experience of co-regulation with our caregivers as they help us with our feelings. We co-regulate before we self-regulate. And yet, if we have not had those developmental experiences, it is backwards: we need to learn how to self-regulate—to regulate ourselves, for ourselves, and only later can we learn how to co-regulate with our partners.

DOI: 10.4324/9781003330950-14

Moving into Working Together and Consent

As we move into working together through exercises that may have a component of physicality and touch, it's important to talk about consent. I've encountered a lot of partners, usually not trauma survivors, who feel grumpy and resentful about needing to check in with their partners about touch, sexual contact, and other triggers that might be more specific to any one survivor. The rationale is—"she/he/they 'know' that I'm not the perpetrator so why am I being treated like one?" However, we need to remember that the body probably doesn't know that. The brain "knows" one thing—this is my partner, and I'd like to find ways to be closer to them and feel safer with them. But the body "knows" an entirely different thing—danger, danger, danger!

Over time, as we have learned more about how trauma lives in the body, how traumatic memories are stored, and how things like touch, taste, smell, sound, sensation, and images, can instantly take us back to a terrifying time, we have also learned that these embodied responses are often very hard to shift. Despite the brain *knowing*, in a thinking words kind of way, that a partner is not going to hurt us in the ways that our perpetrators did, our bodies remember long after the traumas are over. Our bodies try to protect us by keeping us ready to run.

The long-term goal is to be able to think, feel, and respond, in slightly closer proximity, to our *knowing* that our partner isn't our perpetrator to soothe our embodied response of terror. But, for some, that takes a very long time and, for others of us, that may never happen.

For me, sometimes I can tolerate my partner putting her arm around my neck or her hand on the upper part of my back—if she asks first—and sometimes I cannot, that sensation immediately takes me back into terrifying sensations and I need to get that hand *off*! It might be that I'm particularly tired, had a hard day where I got triggered and am really working extra hard to regulate myself and that is too much, or any number of other reasons that my brain and body aren't in sync with letting the shields down for my partner. I'm the person writing the book so, it's not like I don't *know* what is happening, it's just that my body thinks it knows better.

So, even though our brains are moving towards trust, our bodies may still be stuck in the past. For those reasons, and several others, including the kind of modeling we want our children to see and the kind of respect we want to build in relationships, it is important to negotiate touch and bodily contact.

For these exercises, be explicit—ask questions such as:

- Can I touch you here?
- Can I touch you in this way?
- Is it okay for me to be spontaneous as we dance together?

Sometimes just giving the brain a head's up that the body will be involved can keep the trauma in the past and the partner in the present. We will talk a lot more about touch in

Stage Three when we work on sex and sexuality. For now, in these exercises, I invite you to negotiate touch and physical contact in a way that is clear, explicit, and consensual.

Exercise: Square Breathing

Before we move into exercises to build emotion regulation, I want to give you a little breathing exercise that is quick and easy. You can call upon this technique any time you are feeling like you might be feeling "under regulated"—overwhelmed and explosive or, "over regulated"—shut down, dissociated, bye-bye, and numb.

This first exercise is called *Square Breathing*. It is also known as *box breathing* and it is often used as an opening and closing practice in meditation classes, groups for trauma survivors, or classes focused on emotion regulation.

To practise square breathing, simply follow these steps:

- Breathe in for 4 beats.
- Hold for 4 beats.
- Exhale for 4 beats.
- Hold the exhale for 4 beats.
- Repeat.

The rhythm of those beats is entirely up to you. You could follow your heartbeat, the rhythm of the sound of blood coursing through your veins and into your ears, a song that you carry in your mind, or match the tempo to something outside yourself like the chirping of a bird in a nearby tree. It is important for many survivors to keep both feet firmly planted on the ground, to ground you. You might choose to tap a finger on your leg or move a toe along with the rhythm to bring it alive a bit more, to feel more in tune with your body and breath.

At first, you will just do this once, then stop, notice, check in with your body-mind sensations, feelings, thoughts, and impulses. Try to notice if you are feeling more grounded, more rooted in yourself and in the world. Attend to your experience of the exercise. Over time, you will develop an internal sense of when you need more repetitions and when you need fewer, when you need longer beats and when you need slower.

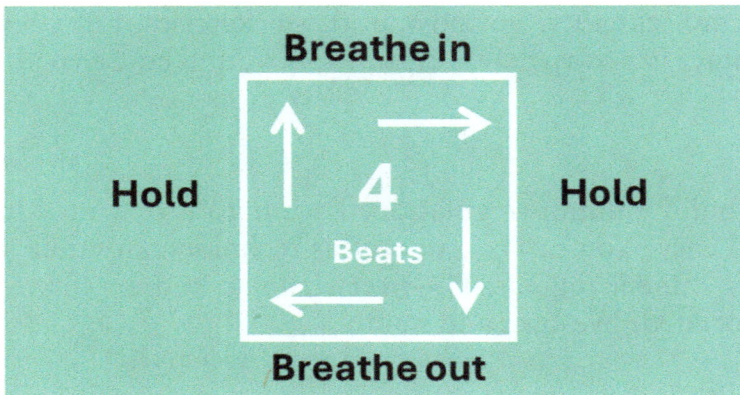

Breathe in

Hold **4 Beats** **Hold**

Breathe out

If both you and your partner have practised this independently and are feeling comfortable with the exercise, you can start doing it together. You might choose to breathe together in the morning and evening as a ritual of connecting and grounding as you begin and end the day. You might also choose to use this breathing exercise before having a conversation that you both imagine might be challenging, as a way of connecting and committing to trying to stay grounded.

To do the exercise together, start in a neutral physical position—feet on the ground, hands relaxed, and one of you can breathe while the other narrates the beat and then, switch. Once you have practised taking turns narrating the beat, try breathing together with one of you tapping the rhythm on the hand of the other or on something that can be heard by both partners. If you are breathing with your eyes closed, it can be helpful to have some physical contact, like tapping on a hand, so that you don't lose one another. However, if that is too triggering, for now, it's okay to just open your eyes and look towards one another at the beginning of each cycle. Either of you can signal to stop at any time using an agreed upon signal like a finger in the air.

It is important to note that many trauma survivors find breathing exercises to be incredibly grounding and helpful. However, there are many survivors who experience breathing exercises as being too much focus on breath, body, and self, and this can cause some survivors to shut down, dissociate, or get flooded with overwhelming feelings. If you already know this about yourself, take a look at the exercise but only explore it up to a point when you notice any warning signs that you might go into a state of too muchness or too littleness.

JOURNAL REFLECTIONS HANDOUT: SQUARE BREATHING

How did you find trying the breathing exercise? Were you the—"Yes! This is great!" —trauma survivor or the—"Oh God, no way! This is way too much feeling!" —trauma survivor?

_____

_____

_____

_____

_____

_____

What did you notice feeling in your body? What did that help you understand about yourself?

_____

_____

_____

_____

_____

_____

What was it like to notice your breathing? What does this tell you about how you inhabit your breath and body the rest of the time?

_____

_____

_____

_____

_____

_____

_____

Did this exercise bring up any strong feelings or memories? If so, what memories came up? Can you share them with your partner? And, was it tolerable to have those memories emerge?

_____

_____

_____

_____

_____

_____

Naming Emotions

The starting point for learning how to regulate emotions is learning how to identify and name them. Many trauma survivors struggle with identifying and naming their emotions and many of us find that we get stuck in a rabbit hole with all of our feelings turning into a muddy, overwhelming, mess. Learning about regulating our emotions can't happen when we are immersed in that overwhelming mess.

We need to start our work outside of those moments, when we are able to think, breathe, talk, and reflect. Sometimes, when we allow ourselves the space and time to tune into our emotions, what we find is a big lump, like—*sad*—a big feeling that is all encompassing. Sometimes, when we allow ourselves that same space and time, what we find is many emotions that feel complicated, confusing, and hard to distinguish. The first step, then, is to take those moments and tune into our emotions, finding ways to name what we are experiencing in *feelings* language.

Looking at the **Feelings Chart,** we can start by noticing the feelings on the left—those basic emotions, like the primary colours, and giving names to our experiences.

To the left of the chart, you can see the most basic emotions basic: *happy–sad–angry–afraid.* Those are like the primary colours of emotional life. From these basic, core emotions, the more complex feelings and experiences can be drawn to the right. For instance, it may not be terribly difficult to name and identify that you are feeling *sad* but, beyond that, it may be very challenging to note that that sadness is built from feelings of *hurt*, *vulnerability*, and *loneliness*. As we become more settled and able to notice those primary feelings, we have the building blocks for reflecting and being open, aware of the deeper complexities of those more subtle emotional states.

DOI: 10.4324/9781003330950-15

SAD	LONELY	ISOLATED	ABANDONED
	VULNERABLE	VICTIMISED	FRAGILE
	DESPAIR	GRIEF	POWERLESS
	GUILTY	ASHAMED	REMORSEFUL
	DEPRESSED	INFERIOR	EMPTY
	HURT	EMBARRASSED	DISAPPOINTED
SURPRISED	STARTLED	SHOCKED	DISMAYED
	CONFUSED	DISILLUSIONED	PERPLEXED
	AMAZED	ASTONISHED	AWED
	EXCITED	EAGER	ENERGETIC
	PLAYFUL	AROUSED	CHEEKY
	CONTENT	FREE	JOYFUL
HAPPY	INTERESTED	CURIOUS	INQUISITIVE
	PROUD	SUCCESSFUL	CONFIDENT
	ACCEPTED	RESPECTED	VALUED
	POWERFUL	COURAGEOUS	CREATIVE
	PEACEFUL	LOVING	THANKFUL
	TRUSTING	SENSITIVE	INTIMATE
	OPTIMISTIC	HOPEFUL	INSPIRED
BAD	BORED	INDIFFERENT	APATHETIC
	BUSY	PRESSURED	RUSHED
	STRESSED	OVERWHELMED	OUT OF CONTROL
	TIRED	SLEEPY	UNFOCUSED
FEARFUL	SCARED	HELPLESS	FRIGHTENED
	ANXIOUS	OVERWHELMED	WORRIED
	INSECURE	INADEQUATE	INFERIOR
	WEAK	WORTHLESS	INSIGNIFICANT
	REJECTED	EXCLUDED	PERSECUTED
	THREATENED	NERVOUS	EXPOSED
DISGUSTED	DISAPPROVING	JUDGMENTAL	EMBARRASSED
	DISAPPOINTED	APPALLED	REVOLTED
	AWFUL	NAUSEATED	DETESTABLE
	REPELLED	HORRIFIED	HESITANT
ANGRY	LET DOWN	BETRAYED	RESENTFUL
	HUMILIATED	DISRESPECTED	RIDICULED
	BITTER	INDIGNANT	VIOLATED
	MAD	FURIOUS	JEALOUS
	AGGRESSIVE	PROVOKED	HOSTILE
	FRUSTRATED	INFURIATED	ANNOYED
	DISTANT	WITHDRAWN	NUMB
	CRITICAL	SCEPTICAL	DISMISSIVE

KW

Feelings Chart

Exercise: Name That Feeling!

You probably aren't old enough to remember the television show, *Name That Tune!* But let's just say, this is the emotion regulation equivalent of that game show. If you feel like you are already able to identify and name feelings, it's okay to skip this exercise and pick up this series of exercises at the point where you start to feel more challenged.

Step One: Identifying and Naming Primary Feelings

For this exercise, I'm going to suggest that if you are working through the workbook with a partner, you and your partner each work on the first three steps independently. It's okay to check in with one another—hey, how's the whole *feelings things* going? But this is the part where you are learning about yourself, and adding a partner can make it more complicated and challenging.

So, we start out with *Self-Regulation* and move on to *Co-regulation.* It's important to start this exercise when you are in a settled and calm state. If you try the exercise when you are activated and upset, it will be too big a leap from where you are now to where you want to be. So, set aside a ten-minute window every day for a week. Put that into your agenda. Assign it a time that you know is manageable. One time I signed up for the free yoga class at the university at a time that I knew would be hard—I only ended up making it to one class.

I was scuppered before I even started. We're going to start with the basics. In that ten-minute window, on your own, I want you to scan through your day and try to identify a moment when you were experiencing a feeling. Then, identify that feeling in the big primary emotions in the Feelings Identification Exercise 1 (Table 2.1). For instance, you might scan your day and realize that the conversation you had with a co-worker at lunch is lingering with you, but you haven't quite pinned down why. In this example, try to tune in to your body, your thoughts, and any sensations that are arising, and find the closest feeling that aligns with what you are experiencing.

Notice if that feeling name, like *angry*, fits with all of the different things you are noticing in your mind and body. Notice if naming that feeling helps bring those complicated thoughts, feelings, and sensations into clearer focus or shifts the experience to something clearer. If

Table 2.1 Feelings Identification Exercise 1

Scan/Identified Moment	One Key Feeling	Scan For Fit	Clarity/Confusion?
Example: scanned day & identified moment over lunch when colleague made a "joke" about my son—has stayed with me	Example: angry seems the closest	Example: scanned my body—anger fit with most of what I was feeling but also some kind of other ick but can't identify	Example: mostly clarity but—also—feels like it's more complicated, more than anger

it does, you're probably on the right track. If not, try another one. Keep going through the *Feelings Chart* until you settle in a place that feels right—trust yourself to know. It doesn't matter if later on you think that maybe you got it "wrong", there really isn't a right or wrong in this exercise, it's just about finding the inside—sensations, thoughts, bodily messages—aligning with the outside—a name for a feeling that feels "right" somehow.

That's all, just identify and name that feeling. We can get more complicated later but, for many survivors, being able to identify and name a feeling is a huge feat.

Step Two: Identifying and Naming More Complex Feelings

After one week of taking ten minutes a day to scan your day and notice, identify, and name an emotion that you experienced that day, let's go a little deeper. This week try to identify and name the primary feeling on the left in the Feelings Identification Exercise 2

Table 2.2 Feelings Identification Exercise 2

Scan/Identified Moment	One Key Feeling — Primary Level	One Key Feeling — Second Level	Scan For Fit	Clarity/ Confusion?
Example: scanned day & identified moment over lunch when colleague made a "joke" about my son—has stayed with me	Example: angry seems the closest	Example: when I looked at the next level, I realized that I was feeling humiliated by this colleague	Example: scanned my body—anger fit with most of what I was feeling but adding humiliation made it feel really cohesive and it made more sense	Example: adding the second-level feeling really brought me into a sense of clarity

(Table 2.2) and then, go to the next column in the Feelings Chart and see if you can identify the more complex feelings that are embedded inside the primary feeling.

Going back to the example of the conversation with your co-worker, you've identified that you were feeling *angry*: that is the feeling that most aligns with your mind, body, and sensations, associated with the conversation.

Now, if we are going to go one step further and walk slowly through the next level—is it *mad, humiliated, frustrated, critical* that fits even more closely with the experience? Perhaps a blend of *humiliated* and *critical* fits best—like a dose of "I can't believe she said that" with a dash of "ooof, now I feel really humiliated and want to hide". The added complexity of identifying and naming *critical* with *humiliation* may bring you into alignment or give you a feeling of recognition. Often, that's enough to help dissipate the sense of things lingering and lurking unresolved. Naming the feelings can help you let them drift away, or it can help you decide how to take action and make decisions about how to address the situation in future.

Remember, feelings aren't "good' or "bad", and feelings aren't things that are "done to" us: they are sensations, thoughts, and bodily experiences that help us understand ourselves and those around us. Feelings give us information about situations and relationships and help us understand more about how to move forward.

Step Three: Expanding Feelings

Step three is another expansion of steps one and two. This week you will extend your "scan, notice, identify, and name" task to the third column in the Feelings Identification Exercise 3 (Table 2.3) For instance, in your conversation with the co-worker in week one, you identified and named *anger* as the primary feeling that was lingering and feeling unresolved. In week two, you extended that to the second column of the chart and noticed, identified, and named *humiliation* and *critical* as the more complex feelings that aligned with your bodily experience, thoughts, and sensations.

This week, extend that to notice a part of you that feels *betrayal*—that person has always been supportive and validating in the past. Also, you encounter feelings of *withdrawal*, where after this upsetting conversation you felt like pulling away from her and others, and feelings of *fury*—things were going so well before that conversation and now everything feels messed up.

Adding this level of depth to your understanding of how you are feeling furthers your awareness of yourself and your feelings, and helps you know more about how you might respond. Might you feel able to express your *betrayal* to this colleague? Is this someone you trust and feel able to share your emotional responses with? Is this someone you have been wary of but continued to connect with because it was easier than pulling away?

Understanding more about your feelings of *betrayal, withdrawal*, and *fury* might help you share this experience with your partner, your therapist, or a trusted friend in a way that helps you learn how to turn to others for support and care, guidance, and comfort. Without a language for feelings, only experiencing feelings as fuzzy things that wander by uncomfortably or as an explosive, overwhelming mess doesn't help you learn how to co-regulate with others who might be able to be there for you and help you plan how to

Table 2.3 Feelings Identification Exercise 3

Scan/Identified Moment	One Key Feeling – Primary Level	One Key Feeling— Second Level	One Key Feeling – Third Level	Scan For Fit	Clarity/Confusion/ Action?
Example: scanned day & identified moment over lunch when colleague made a "joke" about my son—has stayed with me	Example: angry seems the closest	Example: when I looked at the next level, I realized that I was feeling humiliated by this colleague	Example: disrespected— like, they don't know my son, and they should know how hard I try to be a good parent	Example: scanned my body—anger fit with most of what I was feeling but adding humiliation made it feel really cohesive and it made more sense but... disrespected kind of brought it back to the beginning	Example: adding the second level feeling really brought me into a sense of clarity but adding the third level took me back to angry again! I feel like I need to say something because otherwise it's going to fester

respond. And that's the next, and perhaps the most challenging, step: letting your partner or other supportive person(s) in.

Step Four: Sharing Your Feelings

Now that you and your partner have spent the last three weeks naming your feelings, and expanding your ability to notice them, identify, name, and expand them into greater complexity and depth, it's time to share your process with your partner or someone else who feels like a safe (enough) and supportive person.

In this step, you and your partner come together for your ten-minute window. You can alternate taking turns going first or just decide on an order and stick to it. In your ten minutes you will do the scan, notice a feeling, work through the three levels, and do this with a narration that you share with your partner.

As you move into the third column of the *Feelings Chart*, share your reflections on the feelings that are coming to light and move into a discussion to better understand your emotional responses, how your feelings are helping you understand that situation, and how you are learning more about how to respond to the feelings with action—whether internal or external.

After you have narrated your internal process, open the conversation so your partner can share their observations, reflections, and feelings. The partner's role, at this point in the exercise, is simply to reflect what you are hearing, share your thoughts and feelings, and stay focused on the experience of the sharing partner. Then, switch!

Adding to the Challenge

The example we worked with in steps one through three was focused on a conversation with a co-worker. These feelings are not necessarily connected to your partner. When the situation that you feel is important to explore is something that is connected to your partner, that can lead to complications in step four.

We haven't yet worked on co-regulation, which we will get started on in section 2.3 below. Step four is an introduction as we move into sharing our feelings with our partners. However, we are still working on experiences that are external to the relationship—situations that do not require a high level of self-reflection, of regulation—and working through any defensive or reactive responses to protect the safety of this exercise and stay focused on the naming feelings exercise of the partner.

The next step will involve making a challenging leap to sharing reactions and responses to one another and working on staying open, non-defensive, and focused on the sharer. However, we have a little more work to do before we'll be ready for that challenge. Allow yourself to go as slowly as you need to, and make sure to notice your progress. Just because these are skills and capacities that non-survivors may be able to do blindfolded doesn't mean that it isn't a big deal that you are giving yourself the time, patience, and compassion to work on this basic building block of emotional life that you didn't have the opportunity to experience while growing up.

JOURNAL REFLECTIONS HANDOUT: NAME THAT FEELING!

What did you notice in trying to name a feeling for the first time, in this way? Did you learn anything about yourself, how you learned about emotions, and what your defaults are?

_____

_____

_____

_____

_____

_____

_____

Were there particular things you noticed in your mind, body, sensations, that helped you "know" that you were naming the feeling authentically?

_____

_____

_____

_____

_____

_____

_____

Did you notice naming some feelings in the more neutral situation that would have been or were very different when similar situations happen with your partner?

_____

_____

_____

_____

_____

_____

_____

Overall, how did it feel, to feel and to allow yourself the space and time to identify and name that feeling?

_____

_____

_____

_____

_____

_____

Exercise: Exploring Learned Emotional Relationships

The goal of this exercise is to start to understand how our patterns in responding to emotions and emotional situations are formed by our experiences in life, both in childhood and adulthood, and to compare these to our partners. Starting to understand one another and your responses to emotions is a beginning step in building more compassion, understanding, and empathy (beginning mentalizing), in situations that might, previously, have caused conflict.

Table 2.4a Exploring Learned Emotional Relationships: Example

	Family	Community/culture	Traumatic experiences
Which emotions are *acceptable*?	Example: sadness	Example: judgmental	Example: guilt
How do you **cope** with difficult emotions?	Example: avoid emotional talk	Example: using phone	Example: solution-focused thinking
How do you **express** emotions?	Example: in my family no one spoke about any feeling—I never saw any	Example: my friends were comfortable with feeling happy and angry and that was it	Example: in my trauma I had to be stony—no feelings allowed
What are the **benefits** of following these rules?	Example: you didn't get in trouble	Example: no one asked any hard questions if they never saw you looking the way you felt	Example: protected by the stones
What are **drawbacks** of following these rules?	Example: nothing ever got solved and all of the trauma stayed hidden	Example: I didn't feel close to anyone	Example: none!

Table 2.4b Exploring Learned Emotional Relationships: Worksheet

	Family	Community/culture	Traumatic experiences
Which emotions are *acceptable*?			
How do you *cope* with difficult emotions?			
How do you *express* emotions?			
What are the *benefits* of following these rules?			
What are *drawbacks* of following these rules?			

Your task is to consider the role of your traumatic experiences, important people in your life and community, the impact of your family, and how your culture has shaped how you experience and feel about your feelings (Table 2.4b). Once you have completed this worksheet independently, compare your responses with your partner and consider the similarities and differences in your responses.

JOURNAL REFLECTIONS HANDOUT: LEARNED EMOTIONAL RELATIONSHIPS

How does this exercise help you understand some of the challenges you experience in your relationship? How did it help you understand your partner and their responses more clearly?

_____

_____

_____

_____

_____

_____

With these insights, how do you understand more about the kinds of situations that might trigger conflict or disconnection?

_____

_____

_____

_____

_____

_____

How does this help you understand the ways in which you find yourself more able to connect and feel close in response to external situations and events?

_____

_____

_____

_____

_____

_____

Moving into Co-regulation

Now that you've worked on a basic breathing exercise, on your own and with your partner, worked on naming emotions, and started to understand the many factors that impact how you and your partner experience your feelings, it's time to work more explicitly on co-regulation. As infants, we learn how to co-regulate, with our caregivers, before we learn to self-regulate. When all of that goes awry, we need to learn to self-regulate— for ourselves—before we can learn how to co-regulate—with an other. The next series of exercises and reflections is about adding that important piece to the emotion regulation, trauma, and couples, puzzle.

JOURNAL REFLECTIONS HANDOUT: CO-REGULATION

Can you turn to your partner when you are distressed? If so, how, and what is that like for you? If not, what might be making that hard? What is that like for you?

_____

_____

_____

_____

Can your partner turn to you when they are distressed? If so, how, and what is that like for you? If not, what might be making that hard? What is that like for you?

_____

_____

_____

_____

_____

DOI: 10.4324/9781003330950-16

Can you remember a time when you were able to seek connection with your partner when you were already distressed? If yes, what made that possible? What happened when you sought connection? If not, what made that impossible? What happened when you could not seek connection?

_____

_____

_____

_____

_____

Beginning to Put It Together

As we weave our way through first, identifying feelings; next, sharing those feelings with a partner; then, working towards understanding how we have come to understand our feelings and how this impacts our ability to feel safe and close with our partner—we can also start to see how these stepping stones go together to create the ways in which we learn to love and connect with others.

When infancy and early childhood go as they should, and there is no trauma holding you back and pushing you down, all of these steps—woven together by love—unfold seamlessly and invisibly into the quilt of how you become who you are in relationships. When we experience traumas that mess with our development, it is hard, intentional, and challenging to create that quilt. In the end, it's a bit of a patchwork quilt, but it still does the job.

Exercise: Dyadic Emotional Coping, Initial Exploration

So, the next step is to put some of these new insights and skills to the test in your couple relationship. To explore repetitive emotional responses or patterns that lead to conflict and emotional distress in your relationship, we can start by using structured exercises. When an exercise has some structure and clarity, it can help us feel safe, contain the conflict, and give us a clear set of guidelines to direct the conversation and, hopefully, keep us from falling into the rabbit hole of our repetitive argument.

For this exercise, we start by:

- Thinking of recent conflict with your partner.
- Identifying how your situation relates to ongoing and repetitive patterns of distress in your relationship.
- Sharing your log with your partner and discussing the similarities and differences between your responses.
- Discussing possible alternatives to current ways of responding.

The next time you find yourselves in this repetitive pattern, try out the alternative. It's also okay to put these handouts on the fridge, take your partner's hand, walk over to the fridge, take a deep breath, and orient yourselves to your commitment to try something new.

It can feel very frustrating to "know", with our highly evolved brains, what we should do and to find ourselves, time and time again, stuck and unable to avoid the trap of the repetitive argument—that Dyadic Traumatic Reenactment that keeps us swirling around and around.

However, there is hope. As we work more on the cognitive part, as the two of you work together, consistently, and consciously, over time things will start to change. This work is really hard: we are going against all of our instincts, many of which are outside of our consciousness and most of which are outside of our capacity to control. And that is why we need to have a lot of compassion and generosity towards ourselves and our partners as we try to shift these stuck ways of being and doing together—it takes a long time for these cycles to change.

Exercise: Dyadic Emotional Coping, Deeper Exploration

To explore repetitive emotional responses or patterns that lead to conflict and emotional distress in your relationship, *think of a recent conflict* with your partner and fill out the log (Table 2.4b). For example (outlined in Table 2.4a), perhaps you and your partner discussed going to a family event where your partner's uncle, who says inappropriate, triggering things to you, would be present. In discussing your discomfort with your partner, they tell you that it will be more problematic to talk to their uncle or to not attend the event rather than attending and avoiding him. This discussion triggered a conflict that feels familiar and awful.

As you reflect on this situation, use your newfound skills in identifying your feelings, becoming aware that you feel hurt by your partner for not protecting you, afraid that you will find yourself in a situation with your partner's uncle that feels unsafe. This triggers you into a state of vigilance, and, at the end of your exploration of your feelings, you become aware that you are feeling ashamed.

The thoughts that swirl around in your mind as these feelings unfold may include the following:

- Why am I always standing here, waiting for them to take care of me?
- Why won't they protect me?
- They are always running away like a scared kid.
- Why will no one take care of and protect me? I'm such a loser.

Identify how your situation relates to *ongoing and repetitive patterns of distress* in your relationship. As you spend the time reflecting, exploring your feelings and thoughts about this conflict, the repetitive pattern that emerges when you and your partner find yourselves in conflict may become clearer.

You may notice that the fear, hurt, vigilance, and shame that you feel in these circumstances, and the thoughts that emerge in the mess, fuel the emotional chaos inside that leads you to start to panic, to pursue your partner, to yell at your partner, to escalate, and to find yourself in a place where thinking disappears and feelings all mesh into one burning ball of overwhelm. Suddenly, you may find that you can't stop, and your partner has shrunk into a silent "smooshy" blob on the floor, unable to lift their head, speak a word, or be any kind of relational human.

Share your log with your partner and *discuss the similarities and differences* between your responses. When you compare your responses to your partner's you may feel confused, as though the two of you were in different rooms when this discussion occurred. As your partner shares their feelings, thoughts, and responses, it may become clear that the two of you are like a perfectly fit lock and key; your traumas, your triggers, and your terrors fit together perfectly.

While all your feelings of hurt and shame explode into a burning ball of yelling, you may find that your partner's feelings of fear and shame send them into the black hole of nothingness—so far away, so frozen, so completely terrified that there is no reaching them. Your lock—the explosive overwhelming ball of your distress—and your partner's key—the black hole vacuum of silent terror—fit together perfectly.

Next, discuss *possible alternatives* to current ways of responding. As you move into greater understanding of what is happening between you, you may start to reflect on how the past is living in the present in this cycle you are stuck in. Having that greater understanding isn't enough, on its own, to change things, but it is enough to start to see how the strategies the two of you use for emotion regulation and managing traumatic triggers work against one another. For most of us, the thing we want and need is the very thing we aren't able to get when we get pulled into our trauma triggers.

So, for this situation, you and your partner might agree that an alternative response might be for you to do the square breathing exercise, write in your journal about how triggered you are and what you need from your partner. Share this with them, working on your emotion regulation to give them the space they will need to read, reflect, and respond. And, for your partner to try to not immediately disappear or run away, to do the square breathing exercise on their own, and to read what you are sharing with as much openness as possible.

Then, once both of you have tried these new ways of responding, sit down together, talk about the situation with this uncle, and come up with a compromise that allows your partner to see their family and you to feel safe. That might be your partner agreeing not to leave you in a room with their uncle or that you both agree that you stay home if the uncle is going to be there.

In these situations, while it is important for partners to support and protect us, it's also important to be realistic about what is possible. Hoping that your partner would confront their uncle may not yield much fruit—this uncle may not be someone who is safe for your partner to confront. There may be many family "rules" that protect this uncle's inappropriate behaviour. So, when coming up with alternative responses, it is important to focus on the two of you and what you can work on together and not on persons outside of your dyad.

The next time you find yourselves in this repetitive pattern again, *try out the alternative.*

Give it a shot. These kinds of patterns take a long time to change. So even if you can notice the triggers as they emerge, that is a start, and even small changes are changes.

Remember how important it is to note that you and your partner are working together on this difficult way of responding to challenging emotions and experiences—the "enemy" is not each other. You are working together against the pull of trauma, time, and painful reminders of real events that have already happened. We always need to remind ourselves that most of the time we are pulled into these triggers, the thing we are afraid of, the thing we are triggered into expecting or avoiding, has already happened. You have a new present moment each time you encounter these difficult couple dynamics and each time you put even a tiny dent in them, you are healing.

It is vitally important to remember that just because the traumas we may be reliving or triggered into reexperiencing in our bodies or relationships feel 172% real ***right now***, this does not mean the thing that is triggering that response is a traumatic experience in itself—it is an embodied reminder, the calling card to tell you to watch out because something bad may happen again. We really do need to start noticing and putting some distance between the then/past traumas and the now/present/difficult but tolerable situation.

Table 2.5a Dyadic Emotional Coping Exercise: Example

Situation	Feelings	Thoughts	Relationship to repetitive pattern in relationship	Response	Alternative
Example: discussion about going to family event where uncle who says inappropriate, triggering things will be present.	Example: hurt, afraid, triggered into vigilance, ashamed.	Example: if he loved me, he would stand up for me. I'm not worth protecting.	Example: he is always running away like a scared kid and wants me to be okay with that.	Example: exploding	Example: square breathing, journaling, sharing.
Example: my partner promised to meet me at the restaurant at 6:30. They didn't show up until 7:15, didn't call or text, and didn't apologize when they did arrive.	Example: angry, hurt, frustrated.	Example: why do they have no idea how much this upsets me? They must just not care about me at all. How can they be so clueless? I really need to get out of this dead end relationship.	Example: I pursue and pursue and pursue and all they do is run farther away—this time they just totally ignored all of my texts and voice messages and clearly they have no idea how awful it is to feel so abandoned.	Example: when they got to the restaurant I just lost my mind at them. I couldn't help it, I just unleashed my anger and hurt and everyone was watching and they looked totally mortified and I felt like a complete lunatic.	Example: I could have let them know how hurt I felt and how angry I was, but in a less overwhelming way—I'm not actually sure I can do that but that's what I would want to do—to be able to just tell them without having to feel like I was losing my mind.

Table 2.5b Dyadic Emotional Coping Exercise: Worksheet

Situation	Feelings	Thoughts	Relationship to repetitive pattern in relationship	Response	Alternative

It is also equally important to remember that, for many of us, we live our lives embodying our traumas and identities in ways that may spark ongoing trauma. For instance, queer and trans persons dealing with homophobia and transphobia. Or BIPOC persons living with daily experiences of racism and colonialism, reminders of past traumas and dangerous present tense traumas. These experiences are *both* reminders of trauma *and* traumatic experiences in the present. How we may work on the alternative responses will be very different when we separate out the past, present difficult situations, and present traumatic situations.

Regulation and Rhythm

In these exercises we, again, move from individual—self—to couple—co-regulation. This exercise is meant to be fun, connecting, silly, and helpful. We are all different in how we find regulation. For me, music is a lifelong regulating force. In my childhood and adolescence, singing, especially in choirs, playing piano and various brass instruments, and listening to music on the 40-pound boombox I kept next to my bed, were comforts that took me away from the realities of living in my world. Music continues to saturate my sleeping and waking moments, and I have different playlists for different chores, moods, and life experiences—like a playlist for mowing the lawn, a playlist for riding horses, a playlist for sleeping if I'm having a hard time settling, a playlist for writing, and playlists for all of the feelings under the sun.

Exercise: Regulation and Rhythm: Individual

This exercise begins with independent reflection and exploration. The goal is to move from your breath, into your body. Music, sound, and rhythms are ways of embodying emotion and regulation. Finding your voice, your sound, your song, these are all powerful ways of pulling yourself out of dysregulation.

Step One: Finding Regulation

Take a moment, have a listen inside of yourself. Can you feel a rhythm that draws you in? Do you have a sense of the rhythm that feels just right? Try again. Is there a sound, a note, a song, inside of you, asking for some expression? The trick is to listen to your inner rhythms and sounds without going so far into yourself that you dissociate but, going deeply enough that you connect with the parts of yourself that can find regulation.

You'll need to use your other newly developed skills of breathing and noticing to gauge where the "edge" is—the edge of exploring your inner landscape in a way that is expansive and feels centred and gentle versus feeling sucked into dissociation and numbness. This is more practice in regulation as you start to notice these edges and learn to tolerate your own inner world rather than running away and escaping.

If you can find a song, tone, or sound, inside of yourself, let it out—sing it out into the space and fill the sound with the "youness" that is you. Notice how it feels to let the sound resonate inside of you. Back when I was teaching singing and directing choirs, I noticed that almost everyone had a tone or pitch that felt just right—like it settled into their bones

DOI: 10.4324/9781003330950-17

in a way that felt rich and vibrant—and it might not be the same one each day but, when you find it, you'll recognize it as it will feel just right.

If you can't find a song, tone, or sound inside of you that feels "right", that's okay, we can look outside of you. What is your favourite song? Has it been sung by more than one person or group? If so, which one feels just right to you, and why? Pull it up on your media player and have a listen. Does it still feel just right?

Step Two: Regulating

Put on your song. Start humming or singing your own tone or song and inhabit it. Walk or dance to the rhythm you find. Breathe in as you step forward and breathe out with each new phrase or break in the rhythm. Move your body. Add percussion with your hands on your body and focus in and centre into the sensations as you connect the "inside" to the "outside"—the inner voice to the outer reality of your physical body and the space you are in. Always stay on that edge—titrating your awareness to being *in* your body, the empowerment of moving with the rhythms of your own song or finding that just right song on the "outside" of you.

If you find yourself slipping into the fuzzy, numb, dissociation space, stop. Plant your feet firmly on the ground, rub your hands together and orient yourself to something in the space that feels good—whether it's looking out the window at a beautiful tree, noticing your pet's toy on the ground, or smelling your morning coffee—bring yourself back to yourself.

The goal isn't to be perfectly regulated every moment. You can't drive a car in a straight line by holding the wheel tight—it's a lot of little adjustments, left and right, to keep going straight. Our goal is to notice moments of feeling "too much" and "too little" and to find the straight line in the middle, that is self-regulation.

JOURNAL REFLECTIONS HANDOUT: REGULATION AND RHYTHM: INDIVIDUAL

What did you first notice when you went inside of yourself to find a sound and a rhythm?

_____

_____

_____

_____

Were you able to find a song, a sound, a tone, a rhythm inside of you? If so, what did you learn about yourself? What did that song, sound, tone, or rhythm bring up for you? If not, what did you notice, find, or feel, when seeking something inside of you that you didn't find?

_____

_____

_____

_____

_____

Were you able to ride the wave of moving in and out of regulation—like driving the car in a straight line—if you found yourself starting to feel numb or at risk of dissociating or overwhelmed and at risk of getting flooded? If so, what was that like and how did that feel? If not, what did you do to re-regulate yourself and were you able to try again?

_____

_____

_____

_____

_____

Do music and rhythm fit with your natural ways of being? If so, what did you notice when you opened yourself up to the sounds, songs, tones, and rhythms of your *self*? If not, what might be a better fit— art, physical activities, something else?

_____

_____

_____

_____

_____

Exercise: Regulation and Rhythm: Dyadic

Now that you've had a chance to try this on your own, when you feel comfortable and safe in your self-exploration, let's bring your partner into the exercise. It's perfectly okay if you aren't feeling quite safe and ready but you do want to try to bring your partner into your developing emotion regulation. Remember that, when healing from childhood trauma and its impacts of our development, we are moving from self-regulation to co-regulation, rather than co-regulation to self-regulation, as would have happened had development moved along without trauma interfering.

Step One: Creating Space

The first step in this exercise is to set aside time, without distractions—put those phones away! Give yourself enough space to be fully present with the exercise and with one another. Once you have made a date for regulation and rhythm, sit together somewhere that is shared territory, whether that is the back deck, or your living room couch. It needs to be somewhere that you both feel comfortable.

Once you have found the time and the space, come together to talk about a song that both of you feel a connection with. It is important that the words, melody, and rhythm are a "yes" for both of you. It could be a song that you sing together or one that you listen to on your media player.

Choosing the song could bring up a lot of feelings. Music is so intertwined with so many of the rituals and rhythms of our lives—the song that was playing in the restaurant on our first date that both of us said we loved, the song we chose as "our song", the songs we had played at a ceremony of union or a wedding; each song will weave it's way into your body and your connection with your partner, especially if you are someone, like me, who is quite attuned to music and melody. It's okay for the process of choosing a song to be a short walk down memory lane, which could bring up a lot of feelings of connection and closeness and also feelings of hurt and disconnection.

The goal is to stay in contact with words and bodies—holding hands or staying in proximity, in a way that allows you to keep walking that road to finding the song that is just right for sharing together. Try to stay away from a song that has a strong connection with a difficult time in your relationship or one that has strong connections to your life before this relationship. The important goal is to find a song that both of you connect with, together, in a way that feels gentle, fun, warm, and inviting.

Step Two: Sharing a Song

Once you have identified a song that resonates with both of you, sing it or listen to it together, a few times. Share your feelings and thoughts that arise in listening to this song in a new way and talk about what would feel comfortable once you shift into embodying the music together. Are you both okay with touch? Have an explicit conversation about what touch is okay, right down to what body parts, pressure levels, and timing you think will feel comfortable.

Turn on the music or start singing. Allow your bodies to move into the rhythms and melodies and, following your discussion about touch and body contact, dance and sing together through the song. If you feel comfortable, use one another for percussion, clap your hands together, hold hands and dance through the space, breathe together, and notice how it feels to be connected through melody and rhythm.

When the song is over, talk about how it felt to be singing and/or dancing together. I would say that most couples find it a little hilarious, embarrassing, weird, or strange, when they first try this but, think about dancing at a high school dance, this couldn't possibly be as awkward as that!

What worked and what didn't work? Did the touch you thought would be okay actually feel okay, in the moment? Talk about how you felt. Did you feel connected and close? Did you feel co-regulated? What might you change for the next time? Once you've talked that through, even if it's a bit cringey, try again and see what changes.

What we are working for, with this exercise, is for you to have a safe haven to return to and find one another when things are hard—whether it's a word you use to cue the other to turn on the music or start singing, or a text you send if you are having trouble with words. The goal is that you both know how to get back to this place of co-regulation, together, and can call it up when you need it, when things are rough, and you need to get back into regulation. We are trying to build new embodied memories, memories of closeness, connection, and safety—and a little bit of fun thrown into the mix.

JOURNAL REFLECTIONS HANDOUT: REGULATION AND RHYTHM: DYADIC

How did you connect together to identity the song you chose? Does this song have particular meaning for you, as a couple? Was it hard to agree on one song that you could both feel drawn to and connected with?

_____

_____

_____

_____

_____

What was it like to explicitly discuss touch? Did you learn anything new about one another? How was this different from how you talk about touch and body connection, normally?

_____

_____

_____

_____

_____

What do you need to talk about, do, or work on, to be able to return to this song together when you are struggling? What might the signal be that one of you needs to turn on the music or start singing?

_____

_____

_____

_____

_____

Expanding into the Youness

Music was baked into my bones, like the rings in the base of a tree as it grows towards the sun. When I am lost, music finds me. I married another musician, someone who has recorded their music so that it exists for me to find her. I often feel surprised when someone tells me that music doesn't move them or help them find themselves in hard times, as though the very idea of this is impossible.

However, I have no trouble with understanding that there are human beings who like doing things like running and there is absolutely nothing I could imagine finding less desirable. It may be the case, then, that co-regulation exercises focused on music don't work for you and your partner need to find what does work for you. It may be that you and your partner find a way to create together, painting a shared picture with a medium that both of you find settling, going for a run together—ack—or building shapes with clay together. Anything that the two of you can do together that can interrupt a cycle of dysregulation and help you connect and co-regulate works.

Skills Building in Mentalizing

In the first section of the workbook, we started to think about the impact of trauma on couples and mentalizing. Mentalizing is one of those concepts that can take a while to find your way into and understand. However, once you make sense of it, it can be really helpful in understanding yourself and you in your relationships. This concept is a bit like many somewhat complicated things—you take it in little by little, more and more, and then, at some point, it just slots into place and you wonder how you navigated the world before you knew this thing!

In essence, mentalizing is like thinking about thinking and feeling about feelings—what's going on inside of me and how can I imagine and be curious about what's going on inside of others. (If you didn't read the psychoeducation section on mentalizing in the first section of the workbook, this would be a good time to go back and have a read.)

JOURNAL REFLECTIONS HANDOUT: HOW DO I UNDERSTAND MENTALIZING?

What was your initial idea about what mentalizing is?

_____

_____

_____

_____

_____

When you start to think about yourself through this lens, what do you notice about yourself and how your own history of trauma might have had an impact on this aspect of yourself?

_____

_____

DOI: 10.4324/9781003330950-18

_____

_____

_____

When you start to think about you and your partner, what do you see and feel about how mentalizing—when it goes well and when it doesn't—plays a role in your relationship?

_____

_____

_____

_____

What are your mentalizing strengths, as a couple?

_____

_____

_____

_____

What are your mentalizing challenges, as a couple?

_____

_____

_____

_____

How have you, as a couple, struggled with the impacts of difficulties with mentalizing on your ability to work together as a couple and support one another?

_____

_____

_____

_____

_____

Imagining the Inside from the Outside

Mentalizing well means that we can access and explore our own inner world of thoughts, feelings, and sensations, at the same time as being curious about the inner worlds of others. We can also tolerate and regulate our feelings in relationship with others and solve problems through give and take and playfulness. If I mentalize well, my ability to hear and take in your perspective doesn't threaten to dislodge and destroy my own—more than one thing can be true at the same time.

However, when mentalizing is more difficult for us, we can get caught up in not being able to figure out what we are feeling, thinking, and sensing. We can also make big assumptions about what might be going on with our partners without checking in with them or even taking in the cues that they are giving us. When we struggle to mentalize we also can't use our partners as a source of support and co-regulation when we are having a hard time. It is also hard to hold onto our own perspectives and those of another person; it's really hard for more than one thing to be possible—it's either my perspective or yours!

I remember one of my couples struggling with this one. They had both come from very confusing homes where their emotions were seen as dangerous, and they received inconsistent and unsupportive responses from their caregivers. At one point in the therapy, they were very stuck around an issue of "right" and "wrong". The couple couldn't get to a place of seeing that they could both have very different thoughts, feelings, and beliefs, about a particular situation and that that was okay—the issue was really about how to integrate both of their perspectives into a solution that could work for both of them.

I asked one of them, "what would it mean if both of your perspectives were valid, important, and even right?" His response was, "that would be anarchy, I couldn't survive". For this couple, their very psychological lives depended on coming to agreement about who was "right". It took a long time to help them get to a place of even tolerating that their partner could have a different point of view, desire, belief, or opinion, and that could be okay, and even "right".

As we work on mentalizing together, we are learning how to be curious and interested in the thoughts, feelings, desires, needs, beliefs, intentions, and other aspects of our partner's internal world. And we use cues from the "outside" to infer about what might be happening on the "inside". For instance, you might notice that the body language, facial expressions, and spoken words of your partner don't match up—they are smiling but talking about something really difficult, and their body is a bit hunched over and heavy looking. The words say one thing, the face says another, and the body says something else.

As a good mentalizer you might be curious about this mismatch and use the "data" you have about this person to wonder which is the most authentic part of their communication. You might ask them, "I'm noticing that you are talking about something really hard, but you are smiling, and your body looks kind of heavy, what's really going on with you?" This question might open up the possibility for the two of you to talk about what's really going on with your partner or, even, to draw their attention to something they weren't even aware of—that this mismatch is an important signal to their partner that there might be something going on that they need support with.

JOURNAL REFLECTIONS HANDOUT: IMAGINING THE INSIDE FROM THE OUTSIDE

Are you aware of some of the cues that you might give to your partner about how you are thinking or feeling?

_____

_____

_____

_____

_____

What are some clues that you have come to understand about your partner that tell you things about what they might be thinking or feeling?

_____

_____

_____

_____

_____

Take a few moments to share your responses to the previous two questions with your partner. How close did you find yourself to one another's responses?

_____

_____

_____

_____

_____

How did it feel to start sharing these parts of yourself and your ways of understanding one another?

_____

_____

_____

_____

_____

Exercise: Adopting a Mentalizing Stance

We're going to start with baby steps. For this exercise we are going to work on curiosity, perspective taking, and examining assumptions, in a low stakes role play of differences.

Step One: Small Stakes, Big Learnings

For the first step, see if one of you can think of an activity, food, or even something like a movie, that you *do* like that the other of you does *not* like. It can be as simple as you like Thai food and your partner *hates* Thai food. Or you love playing the guitar but your partner hates playing the guitar. But absolutely choose something that is low stakes—not anything that might arouse conflict between the two of you. The goal of the exercise is to explore mentalizing together in a low stakes, low conflict conversation.

Start by identifying and naming your "different like" and sharing this with your partner.

Step Two: Sharing Perspectives

In the second step, your task will be for the partner who is sharing their *like* to explain to the partner receiving the sharing all of the things that you *do* like about this activity, food, or other thing that you know your partner does *not* like. Fill in *all of the gaps*.

- How does it make you feel? (Use the Feeling Chart, if that would help.)
- What sensations or feelings do you have in your body when you are eating or doing (etc.) this thing?
- What do you think about when you are doing this thing?
- Is this something that connects you to others or is it more a solo thing?
- When did you come to like this thing?
- Did you learn about this thing from someone in particular?
- What is your relationship with that someone?
- Does this thing impact how you feel about yourself?
- How does it feel that your partner does *not* like this thing? (Remember, this is a low stakes thing. So, *do not* choose something that has been a source of conflict between you.)
- Add any other things that are specific to your like or loving this thing that will help your partner understand you more and how you feel about this thing.

The stance of the receiving partner is to listen carefully and be curious and open. Try to understand your partner's perspective and try to understand your differences—why your partner's *like* makes sense for them even if it isn't something that makes sense for you. Ask questions, look for clarification, and do your best to stay centred in their experience and in how you are different in ways that are interesting, not threatening or problematic.

Step Three: Receiving Perspectives

In the third step, the receiving partner will paraphrase what they have heard the sharing partner say, in as much detail as they can, exploring whether this conversation helps them understand their partner's perspective on this thing—Thai food or otherwise—in a new way. It's okay to go back, seek clarification, slow down if you find yourself getting a little activated, and start again in exploring this difference, especially if you find yourself down a tangly road of misunderstanding or even feeling confused.

- Share how you thought, felt, believed etc., about that same thing, before hearing your partner explain their experience of the thing, to you.
- Describe what you have heard in as much detail as you can.
- Describe what you think about what your partner has explained to you, in as much detail as you can.
- Describe what you felt in response to your partner sharing their thoughts and feelings about this thing.
- Take a little time to reflect and explore whether their explanation to you had an impact on how you feel about that thing.
- Take some time to reflect on whether you feel that you are more able to understand your partner's feelings and thoughts about that thing.
- Share these reflections with your partner.

You can use this part of the exercise to notice how you are both feeling, share these feelings, to slow down. If either or both of you feel activated or dysregulated, stop, breathe, and rewind the discussion back to the point where things started to deviate from connection and containment and start again.

It is okay if you need a little time to reflect, just set a timer to come back to the discussion in a specified amount of time. It is important that you *do* come back when you say you will. Ideally, it would be less than a couple of hours; it's hard for a partner to feel alone with their sharing and vulnerability.

Even if it feels like the topic is low stakes you are still sharing as deeply as you are able about something that matters to you. All of these exercises require you both to be committed and reliable even if they feel a bit silly or challenging or even boring—you won't really know the impact of the exercise until you've fully engaged with it with your partner.

Step Four: Tag, You're It!

Switch! It doesn't really matter who goes first. I would suggest going with the person who thinks of something first. Flip a coin or play a quick round of Rock, Paper, Scissors. Once you have let the first partner share and the second partner reflect and share their responses, take a little bit of time and then switch.

Exercise: Adopting a Mentalizing Stance

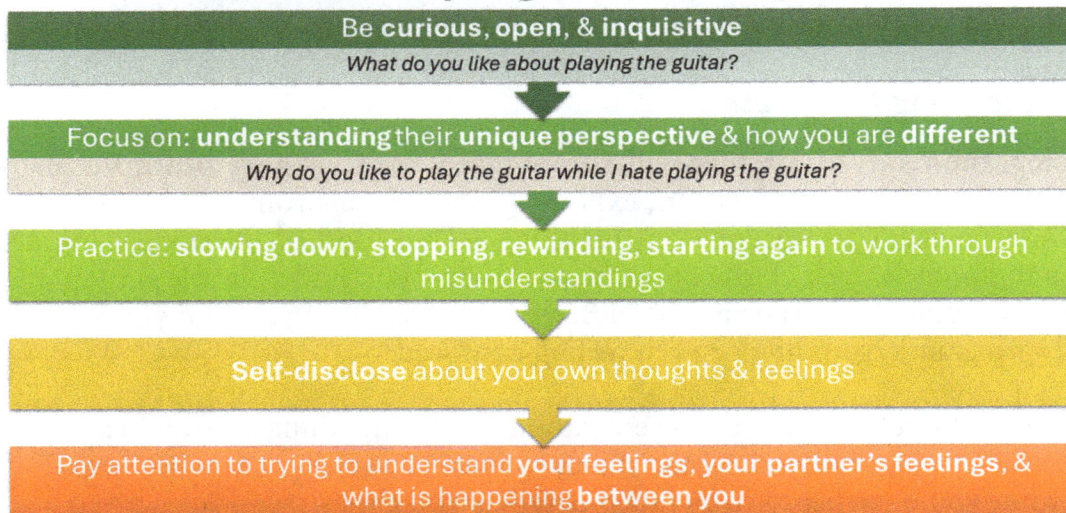

Be **curious**, **open**, & **inquisitive**
What do you like about playing the guitar?

Focus on: **understanding** their **unique perspective** & how you are **different**
Why do you like to play the guitar while I hate playing the guitar?

Practice: **slowing down**, **stopping**, **rewinding**, **starting again** to work through misunderstandings

Self-disclose about your own thoughts & feelings

Pay attention to trying to understand **your feelings**, **your partner's feelings**, & what is happening **between you**

JOURNAL REFLECTIONS HANDOUT: ADOPTING A MENTALIZING STANCE IN A LOW STAKES ROLE PLAY

What did I learn about my partner's *like*?

_____

_____

_____

_____

_____

How did I feel, listening to my partner share about their *like*?

_____

_____

_____

_____

_____

Did my partner's sharing change anything about how I think, feel, or believe about their *like*?

_____

_____

_____

_____

What did I learn about myself and my *like* in sharing it with my partner?

_____

_____

_____

_____

What did I notice about my partner, as I was sharing my *like* with them?

_____

_____

_____

_____

How did it feel to share something I care about with my partner, knowing that it isn't something that they care about in the same way?

_____

_____

_____

_____

Mentalizing Skill Building Exercise

The next exercise is one that you can keep on hand for any time when you are stuck in a disagreement, conflict, or cycle, unsure about how you and/or your partner are feeling/thinking/behaving, or thinking about a past conflict and have a desire to understand what happened.

At first, you may need to take these questions off on your own, reflect for a while, regulate yourself and your feelings, and then bring your responses back to share with your partner. Over time, however, you will become more able to reflect and respond to these questions in real time; that is the goal. You might take turns asking and answering each question and allowing time for reflection.

MENTALIZING SKILL BUILDING HANDOUT

How do you think your partner felt when that happened?

_____

_____

_____

_____

_____

What do you think your partner's intentions were when they behaved that way?

_____

_____

_____

_____

What other possibilities might there be to understand that?

_____

_____

_____

_____

_____

Is there another way to see this situation?

_____

_____

_____

_____

_____

How did you imagine he/she/they felt?

_____

_____

_____

_____

_____

How do you imagine your partner is feeling right now?

_____

_____

_____

_____

_____

How do you understand your partner's response to this event given what you know about the traumas they have experienced?

_____

_____

_____

_____

_____

What did that situation feel like?

_____

_____

_____

_____

_____

How do you understand what has happened?

_____

_____

_____

_____

_____

What happened before you felt so ashamed, angry, confused, or other strong feelings.?

_____

_____

_____

_____

_____

What might have happened for you to feel differently about this?

_____

_____

_____

_____

_____

What do you imagine was your part in that argument?

_____

_____

_____

_____

_____

When you said/did that, how did he/she/they respond?

_____

_____

_____

_____

_____

How do you imagine your partner would know that you were feeling upset?

_____

_____

_____

_____

_____

If this happened again, could you imagine trying something different? What might that be?

_____

_____

_____

_____

_____

When you think about your own history with your family, how does that make sense of what is happening right now between you?

_____

_____

_____

_____

_____

Mentalizing Skill Building Cheat Sheet

Review and answer these questions in any of the following situations:

MENTALIZING CHEAT SHEET HANDOUT

Whenever you are stuck in a disagreement, conflict, or cycle.

Whenever you are unsure about how you are and/or your partner are feeling/thinking/behaving.

Whenever you are thinking about a past conflict and have a desire to understand what happened.

- How do you think your partner felt when that happened?
- What do you think your partner's intentions were when they behaved that way?
- What other possibilities might there be to understand that?
- Is there another way to see this situation?
- How did you imagine he/she/they felt?
- How do you imagine your partner is feeling right now?
- How do you understand your partner's response to this event given what you know about the traumas they have experienced?
- What did that situation feel like?
- How do you understand what has happened?
- What happened before you felt so ashamed, angry, confused?
- What might have happened for you to feel differently about this?
- What do you imagine was your part in that argument?
- When you said that, how did he/she/they respond?
- How do you imagine your partner would know that you were feeling upset?
- If this happened again, could you imagine trying something different? What might that be?
- When you think about your own history with your family, how does that make sense of what is happening right now between you?

Orienting to Mentalizing

As I'm sure you've noticed by now, there is a common theme to all of these activities, that of being curious about yourself and your partner. For all of us, when our traumas wake up and we find ourselves in the struggles of losing our capacities for emotion regulation and mentalizing, we can become completely overwhelmed or completely shut down.

Either pole of this reaction can mean that we lose our ability to tune in to ourselves or to our partner. As you become more and more able to self- and co-regulate and to mentalize yourself and your partner, you will also find that many of these skills become more automatic and less "work". The hope is that you and your partner will develop a bit of a short hand for noticing when either or both of you gets triggered and to flag those moments to slow down, co-regulate, take a deep breathe, and to start again with intentionality—pulling out the *Cheat Sheet*—and bringing your new skills to the task of pulling yourselves out of old trauma responses and into the present with renewed curiosity and clarity.

Developing these skills takes time and intention. When we are little people, and our development unfolds as it should, it also takes time and intention but, it isn't something that is noticed. We simply grow and develop in the context of our families and caregivers who provide us with what we need to build these skills alongside our growing up. So, don't be discouraged if it feels like it takes forever or that change is slow and painful. Remember, it took decades to get here and it will take a long time to reorient yourself to feeling safe to notice your own internal world and to be tuned in and curious about your partner.

A Final Note About Stage Two

I have struggled with how to write this next section. I see many, many couples in my work and most of them are working so hard and with such good intentions. That is the majority of the people I have the privilege of working with. I really want to hold onto that reality, that most people are just trying to find their way to build a loving, close, connected, safe, and collaborative relationship with their partner.

However, sometimes, and I stress that this is a minority of the time, I find myself in the room with a partner that is really struggling to mentalize, but it is also tinged with another quality and intention. It's one thing to find it hard to find your way into curiosity and openness, about your self and your partner, and it's another thing to use misunderstanding and misinterpretation as a weapon, intentionally or otherwise.

I hate the word *gaslighting*. I hate it because when a word becomes part of popular culture it can lose its real meaning and be used in ways that don't really reflect the intended meaning. For our purposes, gaslighting happens when one partner uses strategies to suggest that the other partner's experiences, realities, perceptions, and other ways of understanding their life and relationships are, in essence, wrong. In worst cases, gaslighting is a way of trying to undermine a partner's sense of reality and they can feel confused and crazy.

The term originally comes from a movie called, *Gaslight* (1944) where the husband is, in actuality, trying to make his wife fear for her sanity by gradually turning down the gas lights in the house. When the wife asks if it is getting darker, the husband says, "no", and over time the wife really starts to feel like she is losing her mind. The term has had a resurgence in popular culture over the past few years and it has come to be understood as something that one partner does to the other partner, to intentionally harm them, gain control and power, and keep their partner in a perpetual state of anxiety and fearfulness.

Remember our discussions about emotion regulation, primary and secondary emotions, and mentalizing? One of the causes of getting stuck in leaping to expressing and experiencing secondary emotions is to protect ourselves. We need to protect ourselves from the very painful and devastating experience of the primary emotions, whether they are shame or violent rage, and this leap can also totally shut down our capacity to mentalize. For some completely valid reasons, we have learned that the secondary emotions are the ones we need to live in to survive, emotionally. However, in very severe cases, this can also mean using a kind of secondary emotion–a non-mentalizing tactic for managing how our partners might make us feel or how we get triggered into our own messiness (shame or rage or whatever it might be)—by our interactions with our partners.

Imagine you have an experience with your partner of feeling really hurt by something they have said or done and when you approach them to talk about this, they basically tell you that never happened and that you are crazy. Or imagine that your partner pushes you forcefully, while you are fighting, and you fall and bang your head on a bookshelf and when you try to talk to your partner about your fear of how your conflict is escalating and they tell you that that never happened, "What are you talking about? I didn't push you, you tripped over the carpet." These things can make us feel crazy, and the result is also that the conflicts never get addressed and the partner who is feeling "gaslit" does, eventually, stop trying to address conflicts and problems in the relationship.

Now, let's put this in the context of our discussion of mentalizing and add a dash of emotion regulation and primary and secondary emotions, with a pinch of the shame that devours the traumatized.

Let's imagine again that your partner has said or done something that you found hurtful, and you approach them to talk about how you are feeling. Perhaps, underneath the surface, your partner becomes immediately triggered into feeling overwhelming shame, that shame leads to a sudden surge of the secondary emotion of anger and rage. That anger and rage completely shut down any semblance of mentalizing that might have been available to them five minutes earlier and they explode into a violent denial of your experience—if they can't regulate their shame, they can't tolerate taking responsibility for your experience of their actions. If they can't mentalize, they can't see your perspective and hold it in mind. It becomes a great big mess of them desperately using all of their might to shut down any attempt you might be making to resolve your feelings of upset and come back into feelings of closeness and connection.

Then, let's amp up the volume and go to the second example of your partner pushing you and causing you to fall and hurt yourself. Imagine the force of the shame—for not being able to be in control of their emotions and actions. And imagine the response is violent shut down in mentalizing—how can I hold onto how I have hurt you, in my mind, and still survive without incinerating myself? This leads, in turn, to a total disavowal of your experience—their survival harms your sense of reality and sanity.

So, why am I bringing this up here? Well, because there is a big and important difference between folks who fall into the trap above—losing regulation and mentalizing and losing you, their partner—and folks who are intentionally working to cause you harm, to rob you of power, to cause you to question your sanity, and to take over as the only keeper of the truth.

The first category of human can, with hard work, find their way to changing and becoming more able to acknowledge, tolerate, and respond to your experience. The second category of human will likely not try to engage with change. With the second category of human, you may need to take a good long look at your relationship and discern whether it is safe for you to stay. I'm not saying that that second category of human isn't also suffering; I'm suggesting that, for some, the only way to survive their suffering is to make you suffer.

And the question remains. How do I know whether I'm with the first kind of partner or the second kind of partner? Good question! You'll know by their willingness to work through the mentalizing and emotion regulation exercises with you. You'll know by their capacity to tolerate the discomfort of taking responsibility for themselves in the relationship. You'll know by their gradual change and shift towards being more able to hear you, respond to you, and acknowledge your experience and need.

This can take a long time, but even at the beginning of this journey there is a difference between the first group partner who shows up, reads the sections the two of you are working on, does the exercises, and tries, and the second group partner who may do all in their power to make you feel like a crazy person for even looking down that particular tunnel.

If you are having trouble figuring this out, try to find a trauma-informed couple therapist, someone trained in DCTCT, someone who can help both of you by having an outside and less personal view of what is happening between the two of you.

Attachment-Focused Dyadic Processing

As a young musician, I was never a big fan of playing and singing scales and doing technical exercises; I wanted to sing the piece. Playing or singing the same passage over and over was a bit boring and not nearly as much fun as learning a new piece of music. However, I could certainly see the benefits, as I paid the price in exams or competitions when I wasn't prepared as thoroughly as if I had worked on the more technical aspects of the piece. In music, they say, you need to practise to reach the point where a mistake isn't possible; the music is so baked into your bones that it simply emerges when called upon.

The skills and capacities that we worked on in the second section of the workbook are like that; we need to have them on board even when under the stress of "performance" or, when we are in distress and conflict but still need to be able to regulate our emotions and mentalize. Even now, when I play or sing those pieces, they just emerge from a vault I do not even remember storing them away in. However, I can remember one music festival competition when I forgot my words somewhere in the middle—my singing teacher, accompanying me, took in a huge breath of horror. I made it through, but I always remember that moment of not being adequately prepared.

This part of the workbook is the performance. The first two sections were the rehearsals. And, you can never have enough rehearsal. Sometimes we just need to go back and work on something we thought we knew and then realized...oops, maybe I don't quite have that as well prepared as I thought.

It's okay to go back to the emotion regulation exercises, to go back to your mentalizing cheat sheet, and to work with your partner to build up that foundation of skills and capacities that your childhood didn't allow you to develop. Weaving back and forth between the activities in this section of the workbook, and the exercises in the second section of the workbook, will allow you to navigate the challenges of building a more secure attachment with your partner, tolerate the vulnerability of sharing more about your trauma story, explore the ways in which trauma has impacted your sexuality and sexual relationships, and take a deep dive into how trauma has infiltrated your ways of getting stuck while, hopefully, finding you ways to become unstuck.

Up to this point in the workbook, all of the activities have had both an individual and a couple focus. You did some personal reflection, journalling, worked on specific exercises

DOI: 10.4324/9781003330950-19

on your own, and then, if you felt ready and willing, you shared what you learned with your partner. At that point, you could begin working on the exercises as a couple.

In this next section of the workbook, most of the reflections and exercises focus more on the couple. However, trust your own instincts about your growing emotion regulation and mentalizing capacities, as you work to move through this section in a way that feels empowering and safe for both of you.

We are also shifting the focus from the "top down" work we have been doing in learning about trauma and relationships and building skills, to more trust in "bottom up" insights as we begin to explore, expand, and experience new ways of being, sharing, and growing together. This shift can feel a little scary and a lot hard. Remember to breathe. Remember to take breaks, rewind, restart, and find a slow but steady movement that you can both tolerate. If you find your emotion regulation slipping—go back to any of the stage two strategies or exercises that worked for you; get regulated and grounded again; reconnect with one another; and start again. This isn't a sprint: this is a marathon, so take your time.

And…remember our esteemed friend, shame??…don't let it grab you by the toes and pull you in. Shame is a feeling. Shame is a memory of a time of danger and pain. Shame is not who you are or what you are, it is a feeling, it does not define you. Look into your partner's eyes, if you can, and search for the story that tells you about your strength, survival, and amazingness.

All the handouts in the book are available for download at www.routledge.com/9781032362465.

Attachment Histories Living in the Present

Review

In the psychoeducational section in stage one the idea of attachment and attachment styles was introduced as one way of understanding how we come to believe and feel in relation to others. Take a few moments now to look back on your journal reflections and responses to prompts about attachment.

JOURNAL REFLECTIONS HANDOUT: REVIEW

What attachment style did you most closely align with? When you answer the question, "am I worthy of care?" what comes to mind and body for you? When you answer the question "can I rely on and trust others to be there for me?" what comes to mind and body for you?

_____

_____

_____

_____

_____

_____

How has holding your own and your partner's feelings and expectations about yourself and others, from an attachment perspective in mind, influenced how you have experienced yourself, your partner, and your relationship?

_____

_____

_____

DOI: 10.4324/9781003330950-20

_____

_____

_____

_____

How have you and your partner integrated these attachment focused understandings into your daily life, interactions, and ways of working towards healing and closeness?

_____

_____

_____

_____

_____

_____

_____

How Do We Change Our Attachment Styles and Build Earned Security?

Survivor Couple Attachment Styles

Many trauma survivor couples find themselves in combinations of attachment styles with one partner in the *Fearful Avoidant* camp and the other in the *Avoidant* or *Preoccupied* camp. Remember from the first section of the workbook that the Fearful Avoidant attachment style is basically a combination of Preoccupied and Avoidant styles that swing back and forth depending on the triggers, situations, and emotional states of the survivor. Then, add a partner that is Avoidant or Preoccupied and you have quite a challenging pairing.

These combinations emerge because there needs to be some glue in any relationship; someone needs to move towards the other if someone else is moving away. Trauma can lead to high levels of attachment-related anxiety or avoidance so for every highly anxious partner, there needs to be a bit of avoidance to cool things down. For every highly avoidant partner, there needs to be a bit of anxiety to warm things up and fuel pursuit and reconnection.

In a couple where one or both partners are securely attached, they can balance out times of need and times of independence as they go out to explore the big wide world and come back to the safe nest to recharge and reconnect with their partner. These comings and goings are not stressful or frightening for the couple as they trust that the other will consistently and carefully continue to be there and show up for them and the relationship. For trauma survivors, especially when the traumas were early and perpetrated by a caregiver, attachment security is one of the most significant fallouts. Survivors often end up on either end of the pole of anxiety or avoidance—nothing balanced or easy about connecting with others.

However, while someone in the relationship has to be holding on to connection, many trauma survivors can't tolerate too much closeness. So, having a preoccupied partner maintaining the connection and providing the glue to hold them together works. For other trauma survivors, that special Fearful Avoidant combination of rapid cycling Preoccupation with Avoidance is the only way possible to be "in" a relationship, so they are alternating between being the glue and being the "runner away-er". It's important to remember that both Avoidance and Preoccupation are adaptive ways of being attached that try to help us maintain feelings of safety, security, and sanity in relationships. Our attachment styles are our best ways of maintaining connection—which, to an infant and small child *is* survival— even if those styles don't serve us very well in adulthood.

How Did We Get Here?

If we think about starting to shift our insecure attachments to more of an *Earned Secure* way of relating to our partners, we need to become aware of, and take the risk to push through, our *Internal Working Models* of attachment (IWM). These working models mold our expectations of whether others will be there for us, are safe, and can be trusted to show up when we need them. And they set our expectations for whether we ourselves are worthy of care and compassion from others. To do this, we must do the hard work of looking back at our memories, thoughts, feelings, and even our bodily felt sensations, of how our attachment selves were formed, both consciously and unconsciously.

For me, my adoptive mother was very intrusive, blaming, and also quite vulnerable and insecure herself. The message I got, as a feisty, strong (called stubborn), energetic kid who was interested in everything and passionate about music, was that I wasn't loveable, wasn't meeting her needs, and was very stubborn and willful. Any time I might show any distress I was told that if I was more open, close, and communicative, things would be better. But I knew that this was not true, because every time I did open up in any way, I received blame and shame in large doses from a mother who could not protect me from bullying brothers and a predating father. You can see how avoidance would be the most adaptive way of responding to this mixed message—you are both too much and too difficult *and* you are not loveable and caring enough about me and my needs.

Meanwhile my adoptive father, who had grown up on a farm and, in contrast to my vulnerable mother, was very capable but quiet—in a somewhat scary way—sent almost the opposite message. He allowed me to hang out with him while he was fixing up things around the house, holding the board he was cutting, lifting the stone he was setting, and generally learning about how to take care of a property. In spite of everything, I am grateful for those many lessons as I now manage to survive running my small farm! We played cribbage together, hour after hour, in silence. We went sailing and raced in sailing races along the river, in silence. I learned that I could be close to him and that he could respect and admire my strength and capacity, in silence.

For the first time in my childhood, I felt that there was someone on my side who would be there for me, and I became attached in a *Preoccupied* way; he was there but he was silent, distant, and broody. I wanted to be close to him, but he was unpredictable and inconsistent. I never knew what he was going to do or say. He could as easily give you random advice about managing an ingrown toenail as he could bark at you from moving the sheet (the fancy word for a rope in sailing language) into the wrong position. I felt a bit like a puppy following an abusive owner—you need and want to be close to them, but you never know when you are going to get whacked. When things changed, on a dime, and he became predatory in a silent sexual way, I had to turn the Preoccupation off in a seeking contact way, but keep it turned on in a hypervigilant watching for danger way.

And then, of course, the stronger pole of my attachment style—the Avoidance—was solidified. I couldn't get far enough away fast enough. I learned to leave the house at 6:00am to get away before anyone woke up and to return home after 10:00pm so that everyone would already be in bed. If you look at the yearbook from the years I was in middle school, you will see me in almost every extracurricular club and class; I was even on the cross-country running team—which is hilarious! But, it worked, for the most part, in that I was able to stay somewhat safe in a very unsafe environment.

My Preoccupation shifted to teachers, friends, and neighbours who could provide me with a little bit of care and comfort, even if they had no idea that they were performing these necessary functions of attachment from a distance. It is clear where the seeds of Fearful Avoidance were planted in these two relationships that I have conscious memories of.

And yet I also had a grandmother who claimed me, thought I was funny and smart and talented, and loved to spend time with me baking, walking, talking, and laughing. In so many ways the one week a year that I spent with her—while my family was happily on holiday without me—was a time of security that I tucked away. I don't think I'm underestimating this when I say that this connection saved my sense of my self, my value in the world, and my capacity to love. Without her unconditional love, I'm not sure my Avoidance would have had any room for the quiet and hidden desire for connection that lay dormant in me. She was my only tie to my adoptive family and when she died, I walked away. I now live about 20 minutes from her grave, and it is she whose death anniversary I commemorate each year. She was a simple woman who had been orphaned herself at a young age, along with her siblings. She had less than a grade eight education, and yet she knew so much more about how to love than most people I've met.

For some of my patients, there wasn't even a teacher or a grandmother: they were hidden by their grief and trauma. But even they, as decimated in the world of attachment as they were, had a stuffed animal, a television show, a pet, or a world of fantasy, which allowed for some comfort and connection. There are a lot of children of Mary Poppins and Maria from the Sound of Music in this world of trauma and healing. There is no shame in clinging to whatever life raft you can find; we are wired for connection and, in the absence of anything real and safe, Mary Poppins or Mrs. Brady are very good alternatives.

That short description doesn't include the six months I spent in foster care, where Avoidance was necessary for survival at a deep embodied level. I know nothing about what happened in those months. I do know that I have some physical scars that suggest that things weren't great and that they were possibly really *not* great; however, I'll never have memories that have words or pictures attached to them to explain how my body left those first six months and moved into an adoptive family that didn't get it, didn't understand trauma, and a mother who found my fearfulness and avoidance to be hurtful, rejecting, and evidence of my unloveableness. What I do know is how my body responds to closeness: by immediately shrinking and pulling away, even from a partner who has never done anything but provide me with bodily care and comfort. I feel the shrinking away like it's my very essence, and then my brain says, hey, it's Pat, stop it with the cringing. I'm sure it is hard for her, especially after all of these years, for me still to pull away—it isn't in my mind, it is simply my cells making a clear statement that closeness and contact is dangerous stuff.

We need to become aware of both the experiences we can know in words and pictures and the ways we can *know* in embodied, emotional, and sensory signals, about how our attachment experiences unfolded, to be able to start shifting how we live in relationships now. The goal isn't to be shiny new and Secure in the ways that someone who hasn't experienced trauma might be. The goal is to be the embodiment of the hard work that moves us closer to understanding our ways of connecting, our impulses towards closeness and distance, to distinguish the past from the present, and to be able to communicate about these with our partners in ways that build Earned Security and shared understanding that can create a safe base and secure haven for you both.

JOURNAL REFLECTIONS HANDOUT: YOUR ATTACHMENT STYLE

What experiences come to mind for you when you think about how your attachment style may have developed?

_____

_____

_____

_____

_____

_____

_____

What memories stick out to you as being pivotal in your understanding of your ways of attaching and your expectations of others?

_____

_____

_____

_____

_____

_____

_____

Knowing that most of our attachment security and insecurity is put in place before we are even able to have cognitive memories, what do you feel in your body, feelings, and sense of yourself and others, that might inform you of how your earliest attachment experiences might have formed you?

_____

_____

_____

_____

_____

_____

Also knowing that our attachment security is closely tied to how our caregivers are with us, what do you know about your caregivers' families, experiences, and beings that might help you understand how your earliest days, months, and years might have unfolded, from an attachment perspective?

_____

_____

_____

_____

_____

_____

Who, in your childhood, gave you different messages about yourself than your trauma? Did you have a teacher who took a positive interest in you? Did you have an aunt or a grandma who showed you that you were pretty great? Did you have a pet or a television character that brought you comfort?

_____

_____

_____

_____

_____

_____

_____

When you share your answers to these questions, with your partner, what do you learn about them and how they became the attachment creature that they are?

_____

_____

_____

_____

_____

_____

_____

How has understanding these experiences, memories, and embodied states of connection helped you understand how the two of you became an attachment pair?

_____

_____

_____

_____

_____

_____

_____

Consistency and Change

We tend to be consistent in our attachment styles across our lives—at least that is what the research says. However, while it is very difficult and takes a long time, we can change how we experience ourselves and others in relationships with hard work, persistent reflection and noticing, and taking risks to push through our hard-wired assumptions and beliefs.

Every year, I fill in the same online attachment questionnaire with my students. I've been doing this for over twenty years. I think it's important for therapists to be open about their attachment styles as these have such a big impact on therapeutic work. So, every year, in front of all the students, I fill in this questionnaire—honestly. For the first few years I was squarely in the Fearful Avoidant camp—no budging, right in the middle. Remember, I'm the cooling down energy in my 27-year relationship, so usually I'm in the moving away avoidance part of things, but I certainly have my anxiety and moving towards moments. Over the past twenty years, with a lot of therapy and a lot of living life with a partner who is good glue, I've got one teeny tiny foot into the *Secure* camp. My students are very excited about this!

Another way of understanding this fluctuation is my preoccupation with my sphynx cat, Aliyah. If she is Avoidant—and she is a cat after all—I get exceedingly anxious in a way that does not really befit how one should feel about a cat. I start to fall into despair that she doesn't like me or love me and that I'm not doing a good job as her person. Then, when she does deign me with her presence, I start to feel a little claustrophobic: I can't possibly move if she has gifted me with the honour of sitting on my lap but, somehow, it's only after she lays down that I have a desperate need to get up! Ali isn't my partner, but this does explain exactly how I flip from Preoccupied to Avoidant.

I tell you these stories to illustrate that attachment styles that developed in childhood to adapt to whatever is the most beneficial way of surviving. They can change, but only with conscious effort and work, especially in connection with a long-term partner; clearly Ali and I are still working on this.

JOURNAL REFLECTIONS HANDOUT: CONSISTENCY AND CHANGE

How have you noticed your attachment ways of being changing over time and in relationships?

_____

_____

_____

_____

_____

_____

_____

Making the Unconscious Conscious

One of the trickiest parts of the process of slowly changing our attachment styles is that those IWMs work outside of our awareness. They are a bit like the computer I'm typing on—there's a lot going on inside the laptop, but I only see the words that emerge on the screen. When something is operating beneath our threshold of awareness, it can be really challenging to notice it before it does what it does. It is really hard to be conscious of our unconscious, at least enough to change it. Where attachment is concerned, one of the most difficult things to change is how our IWMs filter out incoming information before it gets a chance to tell us new or different things.

Let's say that Amy, a survivor of childhood sexual abuse (CSA), approaches her romantic relationships with a Fearful Avoidant attachment style. Amy alternates running towards and running away—if she feels her partner pulling away, her anxiety gets fueled and she becomes a pursuer, but if she feels her partner moving closer, her Avoidance turns her into a runner-awayer. Now let's say that Amy's partner, Gale is a survivor of physical abuse in childhood (CPA) and approaches their relationships with an Avoidant attachment style. For Gale, when Amy's pursuit gets heated up, they run as fast and as far in the opposite direction as they can; all of this turns Amy's anxiety into a molten ball of pursuing terror. And when Gale feels Amy's anxiety burn out and she turns to the avoidant part of her attachment style, they become anxious and this anxiety, for an Avoidantly oriented person, shuts them down and sends them away farther and farther from an ever-escalating anxious Amy.

You can see how, when these cycles of trauma-fueled attachment insecurity are activated there is no rest, no co-regulation, no gentleness, and no safe base. Our goal is to help couples like Amy and Gale build that thing called Earned Security so they can begin to notice how their unconscious IWMs fuel their expectations, what they notice and don't notice, and make it so hard to bring about change in their attachment security with one another.

The reality is that over time, across the length of our childhoods and into adulthood, we form an understanding of ourselves, of whether we are loveable, and of whether others will be present for us and how we expect them to respond to us. For survivors, the idea that we might be loveable, and that others might be there for us when we need them, is often unimaginable. Adult romantic attachment relationships are similar in how the unconscious IWMs operate beneath our awareness and perform similar functions for us as those of the systems of attachment we were embedded in as infants and young children. At the same time, adult relationships are different in at least one important way: they are bi-directional and reciprocal. That means that at any time, either partner may be providing or receiving care and support: being the safe base or using the safe base. The good news here is that, at any time, we have far more control over what happens in our attachment systems than we did as infants and young children. We have the power to work, to become more aware, and to change how we are attached within our relationship with our partners.

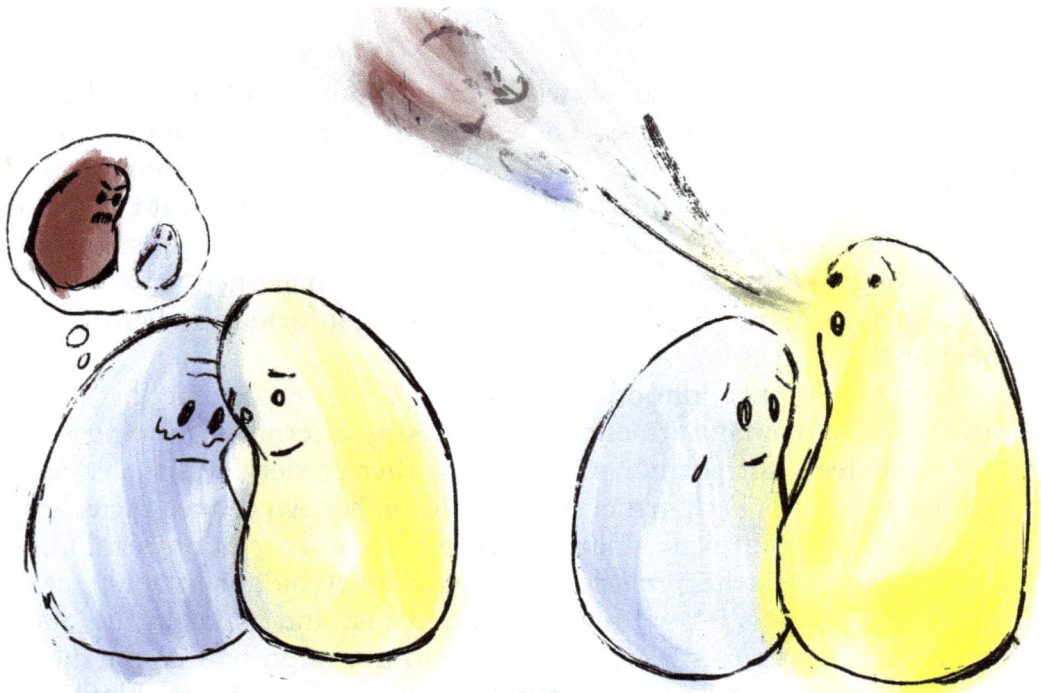

EARNED SECURE ATTACHMENT

JOURNAL REFLECTIONS HANDOUT: CONSISTENCY OF ATTACHMENT

When you think about yourself, what are the feelings and thoughts and sensations that emerge?

_____

_____

_____

_____

_____

_____

When you think about those you would like to be close to, what are the feelings, thoughts, and sensations that emerge?

_____

_____

_____

_____

_____

_____

_____

What does your body tell you about being close to others?

_____

_____

_____

_____

_____

The Change Part! Introducing Secure Base Behaviours

At this point you probably have a good sense that there are a lot of reasons, both unconscious and conscious, why our attachment security and insecurity is consistent across time. One of the biggest factors is how IWMs make it hard to notice things in the world that go against our expectations and incredibly easy to notice things that confirm our attachment expectations. I am very ready to notice any evidence that bad things are coming my way: a shift in a shoulder, a change in the eyes, a lull in the rhythm of the dialogue, or even a whisper of shuddering energy that is almost imperceptible. All of these things can put me on guard. However, I can let all of the disconfirming things go by, like a gentle glance, an encouraging or loving comment, an offer of comforting food or drink while I'm working, or a tilt towards connection. All of these things can wander by unnoticed.

My patients and I talk about the psychic abilities of trauma survivors. We *notice* when something is amiss. The problem is, we often fail to notice when something is positive, good, smooth sailing, and safe. And the other thing is, while we are going to notice the energy that tells us that something is dangerous, we might very well be wrong about what it is that is going on—like when our mentalizing falls apart and we are certain that our partner is mad at us, when actually they are cranky because something went wrong at work.

For our partners, feeling like they are invisible when they are moving towards us in "good" ways but only being noticed when they are moving towards us in "bad" ways can feel discouraging, depressing, infuriating, and all confirming *their* IWMs in all sorts of ways.

If, then, attachment styles operate mostly outside of individual awareness, how can we change how we notice and experience attachment-related moments with our partners? We can try to learn how to respond to one another to enhance security, through changing how we engage in our "attachment behaviours". These attachment techniques, called **Secure Base Behaviours**, are ways we engage with our partners that either stimulate more security or more insecurity. When we follow these steps smoothly and clearly, we are enhancing the security in our relationships and building a Secure Base with our partners. Trying these security-enhancing attachment behaviours, the behaviours associated with building Earned Secure attachment, may help couples gradually shift from insecurity towards security. Sounds good, right? But…it's definitely harder than it sounds.

Shifting behaviours can deal with the conscious, behavioural part of how we connect and attach, helping us do something differently in relation to our partners, showing them our desire to be accessible, consistent, and reliable. But how, then, do we deal with ways of being attached that are unconscious and not related to our behaviours: deep feelings and responses and expectations, noticing the experiences that confirm our expectations, and *not* noticing the experiences that disconfirm our expectations? These silent and invisible ways of being attached can take years of slow but steady work in therapy and in life, with close, reliable, and available others, to come to the surface and gradually change.

However, one of the ways to nudge ourselves, gently, to become more conscious or those unconscious IWMs is to work from the top down: from the cognitive and behavioural parts of attachment to those that hide outside of our conscious awareness. This is no different than how we worked to build emotion regulation and mentalizing capacities in Stage Two—we try to *do* something differently, so that eventually the doing and the thinking lead to more automatic ways of being. We think our way into being and doing differently so that, in the end, we might feel, sense, notice, and experience differently.

This next exercise is a start towards trying new Secure Base Behaviours with your partner. This is a way of beginning to confront those unconscious forces—anxiety about closeness, our urge to avoid an emotionally challenging situation, or the pull away from noticing new behaviours in our partners. Through trying a new behaviour—through doing—we can expose the unconscious underbelly of how our historical attachment traumas cling to our current relationships, while we work on holding onto our emotion regulation and mentalizing capacities to push through to something new.

We are going to try to do something that we learned not to do because it was dangerous for our survival, to try a new behaviour that we have rejected repeatedly because it was terrifying even on an unconscious level. You and your partner will need to support each other every step of the way. Like ironing a beautiful pair of linen pants that never seem to be wrinkle-free, we need to go back patiently, over and over again, until the thing that makes change seem impossible softens or moves aside and the impossible becomes possible. Frankly, I often have no idea exactly when and why this happens, but that doesn't really matter. Some things will never be consciously "known", but any awareness is enough, if it allows change to emerge. Go slowly and bring yourselves back to your emotion regulation and mentalizing capacities, and try to become the safe base for one another while you try these new and terrifying behaviours that we understand to promote attachment security.

The relationship between attachment security and attachment-enhancing behaviours is reciprocal: when we feel more secure, we behave in ways that promote attachment security in our partners and vice versa. To maintain newfound Earned Secure attachment, we need to be good both at giving and receiving, at being both seekers and providers of comfort and support. In the same vein, finding it hard to go outside of our comfort zone and seek support also makes it hard for our partners to provide the support we may desperately need. These ways of interacting become just the normal way we are together, and our expectations for one another become solidified.

Take a look at the Secure Base Behaviours chart. This chart outlines the steps in the attachment dance and how we can build Earned Secure attachment with our partners. These are called Secure Base Behaviours because they are behaviours that help build attachment security and a safe base for you and your partner. They are characterized by their clarity, consistency, and reciprocity. The chart follows a full cycle in an attachment interaction between a couple.

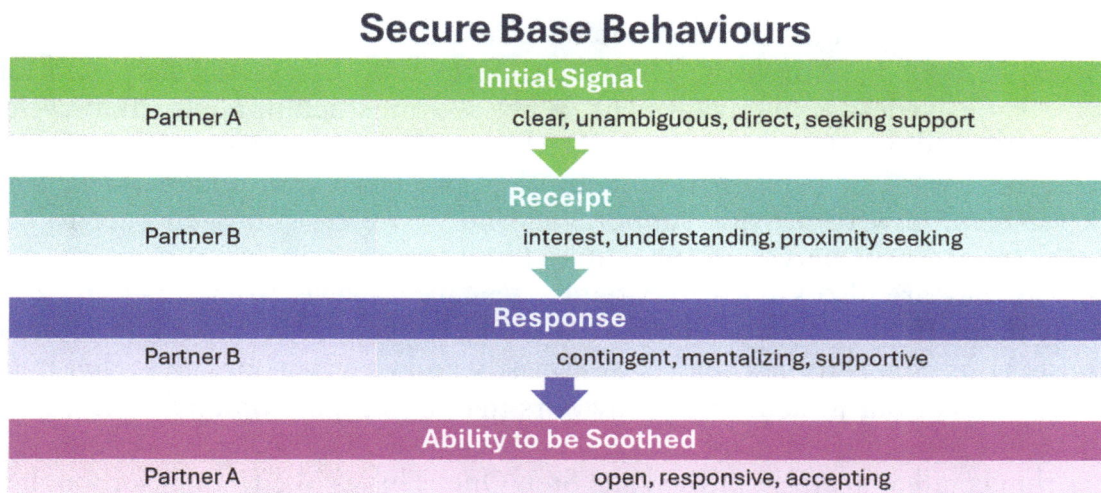

Secure Base Behaviours

Initial Signal	
Partner A	clear, unambiguous, direct, seeking support

Receipt	
Partner B	interest, understanding, proximity seeking

Response	
Partner B	contingent, mentalizing, supportive

Ability to be Soothed	
Partner A	open, responsive, accepting

The *first step* involves a partner giving a signal—a signal about their need or distress that is clear, direct, and draws our partner in to help us. The *second step* involves our partner responding to the signal—coming in closer, showing interest in our distress or need, and trying to understand what is going on with us. The *third step* involves a response, a partner showing that they understand (mentalizing) and that they get it, can help us, and will provide support. They do not get dysregulated, defensive, or critical, or shut down, and avoid connection. The *fourth step* in this full circle of building a secure base together is for the partner that expressed the need or distress to be able to feel cared for, soothed, and helped in their need. They are open, they respond, and they accept the help that is offered.

In my work with couples, one or two steps in the dance almost always get messed up by attachment insecurity and how trauma clings to our ways of being in relation to our partners.

As you might guess, avoidant partners seek support less—step one in Secure Base Behaviours. They also provide less support—step three in Secure Base Behaviours—and respond more negatively when partners look to them for support. Avoidantly attached partners are also likely to avoid conflict, and therefore to avoid the closeness that comes with being able to have healthy conflict with a partner. This then leaves problems unresolved and can result in increased, rather than decreased, levels of conflict in the long run. The *overall goal* of avoidance is to hold our partner at a safe emotional distance, but this can result in even more isolation as both partners' needs remain unmet. Over time these behaviours escalate, as a vicious cycle increases avoidance in both partners in response to less support seeking, and the resulting decrease in support receiving. Anxiously attached partners also provide less support—step three in Secure Base Behaviours—and tend to be less responsive—step two in Secure Base Behaviours and see their partners as needing more support. Anxiously-attached survivors are often seen, in research situations, to offer caring that is out of synch with the needs of their partners. This could be both a shut down in mentalizing and emotion regulation. Partners of Anxiously attached survivors can then increase their level of support to respond to the high level of need, and then they end up feeling more anxious in response to the anxiety of their anxious partner. Around and around it goes.

These Secure base behaviours are behaviours that can be learned and practised and become normal in your relationships. These behaviours are characterized by emotional accessibility, responsiveness, and engagement. When we are stuck in a perpetual cycle of disengagement and unresponsiveness, we need to learn a few new steps.

Trying these new ways of being with one another can feel like a huge risk. Learning how to ask for help, how to provide support, and how to turn to one another to regulate distress: these are risks necessary for you and your partner to shift into more secure attachment, but they are also kind of terrifying. We can, however, sometimes think that we are already doing these things: asking for help, offering support, giving, and receiving. In this exercise, your goal is to first notice, as honestly and clearly as possible, that maybe there are some parts of our attachment behaviours that aren't quite on target for building security.

Sometimes things fall apart right at the gate: Step One. Things like feeling as though our partner should have known that we were in distress—I was crying in the bathroom—but, meanwhile, the partner was out of earshot building a deck in the backyard. If we look closely, in Step Three, we can discover that support behaviours are quickly withdrawn in response to any obstacles. For you to start to make the unconscious conscious and to change these deeply embodied ways of being and expecting and responding, we do have to talk about what is happening between us, but that isn't enough: we have to practise new ways of engaging with one another to break through these powerful unconscious barriers that pull us back to the repetitive ways of being with one another. Those of us with a heavy dose of Avoidance must find ways to tolerate being closer to our partners. Moving towards our partners to seek and to give support can feel very weird and uncomfortable, especially at first. It will take many tries before those of us who are stuck in Avoidance feel safe and comfortable moving towards our partners rather than away. It will take many tries before those of us who are triggered into Anxious attachment will be regulated enough to receive support fully and feel confident in and comforted by our partners.

Helping each other to notice, tolerate, and take in these new ways of being together, as ways of disconfirming old IWMs and beginning to build a new, Earned Secure attachment with our partner, is challenging but so rewarding. Help each other notice in nice ways—not, "hey, you jerk, didn't you notice that great attachment and secure base enhancing behaviour I just did there??"—when our partners are reaching for us; help them find the word and the courage to respond with support.

SECURE BASE BEHAVIOURS

PARTNER A: PARTNER B: PARTNER B: PARTNER A:

INITIAL SIGNAL → RECEIPT → RESPONSE → ABILITY TO BE
                                                         SOOTHED

JOURNAL REFLECTIONS HANDOUT: SECURE BASE BEHAVIOURS CHART

When you look at the *Secure Base Behaviours* chart, can you notice ways in which you might struggle to be clear and consistent, supportive and responsive in your ways of connecting with your partner?

_____

_____

_____

_____

_____

_____

_____

Do you find *Step One*—sending a clear signal—challenging? If so, how?

_____

_____

_____

_____

_____

_____

_____

Do you find **Step Two**—receiving and moving closer to your partner—challenging? If so, how?

_____

_____

_____

_____

_____

_____

Do you find **Step Three**—responding and supporting—challenging? If so, how?

_____

_____

_____

_____

_____

_____

Do you find **Step Four**—receiving and accepting support and care—challenging? If so, how?

_____

_____

_____

_____

_____

_____

_____

If you were to answer the same questions, as above, in thinking about how your partner experiences these steps, where would you see them struggling? How do you know this? What are the signs you *do* notice?

_____

_____

_____

_____

_____

_____

_____

Can you think of cues that you might be *not* noticing that would disconfirm your IWMs?

_____

_____

_____

_____

_____

_____

What are the cues that you might be more likely to notice that would confirm your IWMs?

_____

_____

_____

_____

_____

_____

_____

If you were to answer the last two questions in relation to your partner's noticing and not noticing, what might you think?

_____

_____

_____

_____

_____

_____

_____

Exercise: Secure Base Behaviours

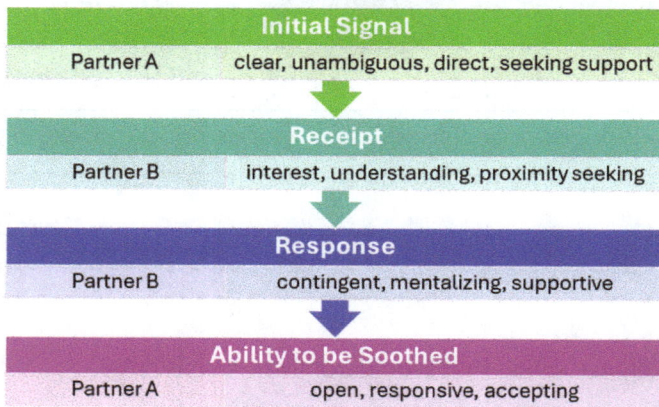

Exercise: Secure Base Behaviours

Initial Signal	
Partner A	clear, unambiguous, direct, seeking support

Receipt	
Partner B	interest, understanding, proximity seeking

Response	
Partner B	contingent, mentalizing, supportive

Ability to be Soothed	
Partner A	open, responsive, accepting

Ways of engaging that foster attachment security

STEP 1:

Look at your negative cycle and identify one "link" on the attachment chain where you get stuck.

STEP 2:

Identify link to early developmental attachment experiences.

STEP 3:

Identify strategies for consciously addressing these mostly unconscious processes.

First Run Through

Let's give this exercise a try. For a first run through, choose a situation that has already happened where you and your partner fell down at being able to "do" the steps above. Do your best to find an interaction that isn't too loaded with pain and conflict. Perhaps you needed your partner to pick up a prescription from the pharmacy, and things got all confused and messed up and you ended up feeling let down and your partner ended up feeling like they were being blamed unfairly for not getting the message about how important this was to you. Let's see if we can find the places in the secure base behaviour chain where our attachment IWMs and struggles got in the way.

Step One: Identifying the Weak Link in the Sequence

SECURE BASE BEHAVIOURS EXERCISE STEP ONE: IDENTIFYING THE WEAK LINK IN THE SEQUENCE HANDOUT

In the the first step of this exercise you and your partner are going to see if you can identify where in the sequence of Secure Base Behaviours that you, individually and as a couple, have weak links in the chain of attachment. For this exercise, I will refer to the person sending a signal for support as the **Support Seeking Partner** and the partner who is receiving and responding to this signal for support as the **Support Request Receiving Partner**.

When you think back on the interaction you chose to explore, did you, if you were the support seeking partner, ask clearly for what you needed and explain the who, what, where, when, and whys? Using our example, did you tell your partner that you needed them to pick up the prescription because you were going to be in an unchangeable meeting all day and that you were down to your last pill? Were you clear? Were you specific? Were you direct? If you feel that you were, how would you describe this to your partner to help them understand what that looked like for you?

_____

_____

_____

_____

_____

_____

If you were not clear, direct, and specific, what do you now notice in how you sought support that didn't quite fit the clear, specific, and direct qualities of a strong support seeking request?

_____

_____

_____

_____

_____

_____

For the support request receiving partner, if your partner has explained how they feel that they were clear in their request for support, what might you have or have not noticed? How did this feel? What do you remember thinking, feeling, sensing, and responding, to this request?

_____

_____

_____

_____

_____

_____

_____

If you did not feel that your partner was clear, direct, and specific in their request for support, how would you characterize the request? Were you aware that there was a request? What did you notice? What, in hindsight, do you now realize that you didn't notice?

_____

_____

_____

_____

_____

_____

For the support request receiving partner, how do you feel you "did" with **Step Two**? Do you feel that you responded with interest, understanding, and moving closer?

_____

_____

_____

_____

_____

_____

_____

What do you notice about what you noticed in your partner's request for support?

_____

_____

_____

_____

_____

_____

_____

For the support seeking partner, what do you notice about how your partner responded to your request for care?

_____

_____

_____

_____

_____

_____

_____

And, for the support seeking partner, how do you feel you "did" with accepting the support offered and/or received from your partner? Were you able to accept the care? Did you move closer to them? If not, how did you avoid receiving the care? How did you wiggle away?

_____

_____

_____

_____

_____

_____

_____

How do both of you feel now that you are reviewing this situation? What are your sensations, thoughts, and feelings?

_____

_____

_____

_____

_____

_____

_____

What do you both notice as having been the same or different from your attachment dance in the past?

_____

_____

_____

_____

_____

_____

_____

For these questions, we were first working with a low stakes situation, like picking up a prescription at the pharmacy. However, that doesn't mean that some of the stress cracks in your attachment might not have shown up.

In your shared discussion, did you notice places in those four attachment steps where strong emotions came up, where you *did* or *did not* notice an important signal from your partner, or wiggled closer or further away in response to your partner?

_____

_____

_____

_____

_____

_____

_____

Step Two: Identifying the Link to Early Development

In the second step of this exercise, your goal is to identify experiences, memories, relationships, and traumatic whispers (or shouts) from the past that are clinging to your relationship in the present and getting in the way of you being able to fully engage in Secure Base Behaviours.

This is one way to start to understand how we can get stuck in attachment sequences that don't result in feeling safer, closer, and connected and why it can be so hard for us to do things that are seemingly "so easy". We will try to identify links to early attachment experiences and traumas that might be a part of the *why* of how things get messy in your bids to connect with your partner.

When we think of the first step, perhaps upon deeper reflection you realized that an early experience interferes with your ability to tolerate and fully embrace making a clear, direct, and specific request for support. Perhaps you remember that whenever you asked for something, for support, or for contact, during childhood, that you were shamed, made fun of, ridiculed, or even abused. Feeling that asking for support would lead to abuse, and not result in receiving the support that you needed, would make perfect sense of why it is hard for you now to ask for what you need from your partner in clear, direct, and specific ways. Perhaps you felt ashamed of your distress when you were growing up, especially when your mother made fun of you for crying. Perhaps you simply learned never to ask for help and that you should hide yourself away and cry in solitude. But, through exploring and reflecting on these interactions, maybe you can start to nudge that automatic pull-away to isolation into noticing when you find yourself slipping away when you are distressed. Through hard work and reflection—and noticing how uncomfortable it is to work against the automatic IWMs that have become "normal" and to try something different—you can try to practise telling your partner when you need their support, even around small things so that you can get used to what that might be like.

One of my most vivid very early memories is of sitting in the grocery cart—you know, in that little front space where little people get plopped and can dangle their feet—in a store. I was probably three or four years old. My cousin, who was three days older than me, and who I loved, loved, loved, was asking for something at the store: no drama but a clear, direct, and specific request to her caregiver, my aunt. My mother was disgusted by my cousin's request. She whispered to me in a conspiratorial way that only bad girls asked for things and that I was being a good girl, sitting quietly and not asking for anything. It was a moment that is frozen in my mind and body. My mother never told me that there was anything good about me so the message was clear: this *one* thing that you *didn't* do was the *only* thing that is good about you. Imagine being three years old and finding out that the only way to be approved of and to have the approval of your adopted mother, who told you that you were not loveable and were very bad, was to never ask for anything. Oof. It worked…I never ask for anything. I am incredibly self-sufficient and will spend weeks underneath my broken tractor before asking for help. Not only does this waste a lot of time and energy, it also perpetuates my belief that I am alone in the world and that no one *will* help me.

We call those moments **Model Scenes** because they become stamped on our selves as models, like our IWMs, for how to be, how to connect, and how to relate to the attachment people in our lives. These are the whispers that linger in our beings and that conspire with all of the other stories we hold to be the stick in the spoke of our Secure Base Behaviours as we try, try, try again, to build Earned Security with our partners. These reflections help us identify the link in this attachment sequence that might fall apart, and more importantly *why*. What are we noticing and not noticing? What memories, feelings, sensations, impulses, and thoughts are hijacking our ability to be fully *in* the Secure Base sequence?

SECURE BASE BEHAVIOUR EXERCISE STEP TWO: IDENTIFYING THE LINK TO EARLY DEVELOPMENT HANDOUT

What memories, experiences, bodily sensations or other whispers are you noticing as you reflect on struggles you may have in **Step One** of the **Secure Base Behaviours** sequence? For instance: I am distressed, I am crying in my room, I am upset that my partner is not responding—but my partner is not within hearing range and doesn't actually know that I am distressed—so, my "signal" is not clear, direct, and support seeking.

_____

_____

_____

_____

_____

_____

_____

What do you notice about your partner in their ways of asking and sending you messages about their needs and distress?

_____

_____

_____

_____

_____

_____

Often couples are puzzle pieces and the person who is going to fit into your puzzle is often the person who fills a slot in your incomplete puzzle. In the beginning, it feels good and refreshing but, as time moves along, it can morph into something that feels triggering, scary, or even dangerous. So, while one of you may feel comfortable expressing needs, desires, and distress, the other one of you may find it incredibly hard, bordering on impossible, to ever make a clear, direct, and specific signal for support and care. My partner is able to ask for what she needs in clear, direct, and specific ways and it terrifies me. How refreshing to not have to guess. How terrifying that she is breaking *all* of the rules.

Have you started to notice themes in how the two of you interact when one partner makes a clear, direct, and specific signal for support? What are the puzzle pieces that the two of you provide to one another? How do your stories collide to create the perfect storm when it comes to the first step of making the signal?

_____

_____

_____

_____

_____

_____

Moving to the **Step Two** in the **Secure Base Behaviour** sequence—**Receipt**—what did you notice about how you, if you were the support request receiving partner, felt, thought, and experienced, the request? What memories, feelings, experiences, and traumatic sensations come up for you when your partner needs something from you?

_____

_____

_____

_____

_____

_____

_____

If you were the support seeking partner, what did you notice about how you were (or were not) able to notice, attend, and feel, in your partner as they received your request? Did you notice your partner embodying the **Secure Base Behaviours** of Receipt showing you that they _did_ receive your signal by moving towards you, seeking clarification and understanding, showing interest in meeting your need? If not, what did you notice? What signals might you have noticed that suggested to you that they _did not_ receive your signal?

_____

_____

_____

_____

_____

_____

What memories, feelings, experiences, and traumatic sensations come up for you when your partner is receiving your request for support? Are there memories, experiences, traumatic whispers that help you understand what might make it _hard_ for you, or _easy_, to notice, tolerate, and engage with, your partner's response to your need?

_____

_____

_____

_____

_____

_____

_____

Moving to the third step in the *Secure Base Behaviour* sequence—**Response**—what did you notice about how you, if you were the support request receiving partner, felt, thought, and experienced, as you shifted from Receipt to Response? What memories, feelings, experiences, and traumatic sensations come up for you when you are responding to your partner's signals for care?

_____

_____

_____

_____

_____

_____

What did you notice about how you, if you were the support seeking partner, were able, or not able, to notice, attend, and feel, in your partner as they responded to your request? Did you notice your partner embodying the *Secure Base Behaviours* of Response showing you that they *did* receive and respond to your signal by responding in a way that fit with what you needed, showed that they understood what you needed, and clearly demonstrated support for you? If not, what did you notice? What signals might you have noticed that suggested to you that they *did not* receive and respond to your signal?

_____

_____

_____

_____

_____

_____

_____

What memories, feelings, experiences, and traumatic sensations come up for you when your partner is responding to your request for support? Are there memories, experiences, traumatic whispers that help you understand what might make it *hard* for you, or *easy*, to notice, tolerate, and engage with, your partner's response to your need?

_____

_____

_____

_____

_____

_____

Moving to the fourth step in the **Secure Base Behaviour** sequence—**Ability to Be Soothed**—what did you notice about how you, if you were the support request receiving partner, felt, thought, and experienced, your partner as they received your response? Did your partner receive your support with openness, and did they appear to **receive your support as soothing** and regulating? Did your partner appear to **struggle to receive your support** and receive your support as soothing and regulating? What memories, feelings, experiences, and traumatic sensations come up for you when your partner *was* or *was not* soothed by your response?

_____

_____

_____

_____

_____

_____

If you were the support seeking partner, what did you notice about how you *were* (or *were not*) able to notice, attend, and feel, in your partner as they responded to your request? Did you notice anything—sensation, memory, feeling, thought—that ran in and screamed **"Stop!!! Don't do it!"** when you were trying to receive your partner's response and openly accept and feel soothed by their response? Or did you notice anything—sensation, memory, feeling, thought, or impulse—that moved you towards your partner with openness, acceptance, and a feeling of being soothed?

_____

_____

_____

_____

_____

_____

_____

What memories, feelings, experiences, and traumatic sensations come up for you when you are receiving or giving support? Are there memories, experiences, traumatic whispers that help you understand what might make it *hard* for you, or *easy*, to notice, tolerate, and engage with, your partner, to be open, responsive, accepting and to feel soothed?

_____

_____

_____

_____

_____

_____

_____

Step Three: Strategies for Change

The following strategies are a beginning point for making change and learning how to strengthen your Secure Base Behaviours to begin to build your Earned Security together. These exercises may feel weird or uncomfortable but they are the building blocks for a new way of closeness and connection.

Flipping the Sequence

Once you have done a full run through of the reflections and journalling prompts for the first two steps of the Secure Base Behaviours exercise, with one partner in the support seeking role and the other partner in the support request receiving role, it's time to flip things over. Find another example, something recent, clear, and not emotionally loaded with all of the conflicts you've ever had and do the exercises again while reflecting about being in the opposite role in the sequence.

Sharing

If, up to now, you have been doing this exercise on your own, it's time to take the risk to share your responses with your partner. Go step by step, question by question, and slowly share your responses with one another. As in our work with emotion regulation and mentalizing, it is important to listen, reflect, breathe, and respond. If you are having trouble regulating yourself—especially if you feel your partner is *not* mentalizing in their reflections about you and your thoughts, feelings, responses, and behaviours, it's okay to say something like, "I just need to take a breather, could we do the Square Breathing Exercise?" and bring yourselves back into contact and regulation. It's also okay, once your partner has finished sharing, to tell them that you experienced that step in the Secure Base Behaviour Sequence differently than they did. It's not your role to tell your partner that they are wrong or off base about how they experienced themselves, but it is okay to let them know about you—how you experienced the step in the sequence that they are sharing with you.

A lot of couple therapists focus on something called *"I" language*. In essence, if you start to hear yourself saying things like *you* did this or *you* were wrong, or *you* felt this, it's important to step back, do a scan of yourself and your emotional state, check in with your own self as a mentalizing partner, and then move into I statements—I believe that this is what I did or I felt this at that moment, I was thinking this at this point in the exercise. After this, it is important to ask them to move into their I statements as you take another run at a more conflictual point in the sequence.

Continuing the Exploration

Now that you have started reflecting on what you *do* and *do not* notice, feel, and experience, *do* and *not do* in Secure Base Behaviour sequences, you can begin to apply this exercise to your daily relationship life. When you find yourselves getting stuck in a conflict that echoes some of these missteps and missed links in the Secure Base Behaviour sequence, use the handout above to work your way through what happened—using those I statements and all the emotion regulation and mentalizing capacities you have worked so hard for!—to go, step by step, and to notice what you *do* and *do not* notice, where the missed step is in connecting, comforting, communicating, and moving from signal to response to soothing.

Over time, it will become more and more comfortable to walk through these steps, to have more of an expectation of what might be difficult based on all of your reflecting, sharing, and understanding, and to start to notice the things you used to *not* notice, to have more compassion for our partners as we understand more about the reasons for their struggles, and to build that Earned Security that we all long for.

Disclosure

Telling the Stories

This next section of the workbook is, perhaps, the least complicated of all the sections and yet, perhaps, one of the hardest. In my early research, I quite unexpectedly found that the couples who disclosed more of their stories—painful stories of trauma, betrayal, and abuse—had better outcomes in relation to their couple satisfaction and trauma symptoms. Basically, couples who shared more, became closer. And partners who shared more felt less "traumatized". What that looks like is less avoidance of trauma triggers, fewer flashbacks and nightmares, and more ease and emotion regulation. I know that doesn't sound like any version of rocket science but, in a way, it was a surprise.

We don't think anything about wanting to know all about our partner's life, self, family, work, friends, and so on. But somehow, when it comes to sharing our traumas, it feels like those are off limits, too private, maybe even dangerous to share. And then, there's our old nemesis—*shame*—showing up on the regular and poking its head in where it doesn't belong. Cultural, social, familial, emotional, and so many other learned "rules" can keep us from sharing the most vulnerable and painful parts of our lives. And this, in turn, can keep us from finding ways to feel safely connected and close to our partners.

In my practice, I have stopped being surprised by how little partners know about one another's trauma stories. Usually they know the title—childhood sexual abuse, for instance. Sometimes they know the *when*—from ages eight to twelve. Sometimes they know the *who*—Uncle Frank and Cousin Bella. But rarely do they know the *what*—the things that actually happened, the memories, the sensations, the feelings, and the ways in which these traumatic events have shaped what we think and feel about ourselves and others.

Disclosing Beyond the Title of the Story

In my research examining how sexual abuse survivors found ways to disclose to partners about their trauma experiences, some gender differences emerged in how and why survivors share with their partners. Women are more likely to disclose the "title" of their trauma to their partners early on in the relationship, because they feel that their partners should know that they are getting "damaged goods". Male survivors, on the other hand, reported to us that they often only tell their partners when they have no choice, such as when the police are knocking on the door looking for testimony in a large-scale abuse case.

I can remember one man telling me about what was happening in his mind when he saw the police walk up to his front door. In the media, he had noticed the growing scope

DOI: 10.4324/9781003330950-21

of an investigation against the organization in which his sexual abuse had occurred. His response was to shrink further and further away, hoping he would not be drawn in or questioned. As the police were walking up to the front door of the home he shared with his partner of many years, he realized he'd have to tell her now.

Another male survivor, of South Asian cultural background, only disclosed about his abuse to his wife of over twenty years when she threatened to leave him. For years she had felt disconnected and unwanted emotionally or sexually. He felt forced to disclose this deeply disturbing and shameful experience that, for him, felt more like something that *was* him and not something that had *happened to* him. Making this disclosure saved their relationship: his wife began to understand his distance, his sexual difficulties, and his avoidance of intimacy. She was mad, hurt, and felt furious about how many years had been lost, but she was also able to understand why he felt he could not disclose. She recognized how this was connected to the cultural and familial values of being the eldest son, the "strong" male figure for his parents' hopes and his siblings' care.

Unsurprisingly, there is little to no research on the disclosure experiences of trans and non-binary trauma survivors. However, in my clinical practice, I have experienced the confusion and complexity that knot together the many factors tied up in trans and non-binary survivors' trauma. Experiences of body dysmorphia (dysmorphia means discomfort or feeling like a body isn't okay or comfortable), and gender dysphoria (dysphoria meaning real discomfort to the point of being emotionally painful), connect to the ways trans and non-binary children and youth feel they have a secret, sometimes a shameful secret, if they don't have caregivers to whom they can disclose their gender identity. And then, if they do disclose their gender identity to caregivers, experiences of trauma can be turned around, "explained" by the trans or non-binary identity as though they were prey to perpetrators because of their gender identity.

A similar theme comes up for LGBQ survivors. Queer survivors can feel confused about how their sexuality might be "caused" by sexual abuse by a same sex perpetrator—this is a fear especially among cisgender gay male survivors of sexual abuse by other cisgender men. For lesbian and bisexual cisgender female survivors of sexual abuse, almost the opposite is true. There is a cultural belief, unspoken but definitely "in the well water", that a woman might become a lesbian because they were sexually abused by a man, and therefore they "choose" to avoid men sexually. With almost 40% of women reporting that they have experienced some form of sexual violence before the age of 18, mostly perpetrated by men, if this "caused" women to become lesbian or bisexual a lot more that 10% of the population of women would be in the lesbian/bisexual camp!

DISCLOSING THE TITLE OF YOUR TRAUMA STORY HANDOUT

How and why did you make a disclosure about the "title" (physical, sexual, emotional abuse, etc.) of your traumas to your partner?

_____

_____

_____

_____

_____

_____

_____

How did your partner disclose to you? How did that feel? What were your thoughts?

_____

_____

_____

_____

_____

_____

How did your partner respond to your disclosure or you to theirs?

_____

_____

_____

_____

_____

_____

How much does your partner know about the "what"—the details of what actually happened—of your trauma?

_____

_____

_____

_____

_____

_____

_____

How much do you imagine you know about your partner's "what"?

_____

_____

_____

_____

_____

_____

Going Deeper and Growing Closer

Keeping secrets creates distance, a barrier against letting down your guard lest something seep out; it also brings shame and challenges with closeness. In the short run, disclosure can feel impossible, shameful, frightening, and risky: "what if my partner really does find out how damaged I am and leaves me?" Safely talking through traumas and sharing these stories with someone close to you increases feelings of competence, decreases trauma symptoms, decreases shame, and increases intimacy in the long run. In spite of the sense of risk and the feelings of fear, we need to share more of our stories to find ways to allow our partners to be the safe haven and secure bases that we so desperately long for—and at the same time, fear.

Each step in healing your relationship, while healing yourself, is a process of breaking down the barriers of avoidance created by the ravages of a traumatic childhood where sharing, being close, trusting, and intimacy could be deeply dangerous. To get there, it is essential to break down secrets between you and your partner, including secrets related to your traumas. Avoidance is the number one factor that keeps trauma and emotion regulation challenges and attachment insecurity fired up and feeling like forever.

We tell these trauma stories so that our partners will come to understand the scope and magnitude of your traumas and become more able to empathize and mentalize about you, especially in understanding more about how these experiences continue to spill into areas of ongoing pain and struggle between you.

Understanding more about the specifics of the trauma also helps your partner make sense of your trauma triggers and some of the attachment IWMs that impact what you *do* and *do not* notice. How you attend to aspects of your partner can confirm your expectations of danger and betrayal while hiding from us the ways that your partner shows you that they are safe, present, willing, and ready to be a safe base for you.

For many survivors, a trauma narrative runs through our lives. Perhaps trauma began before our earliest conscious memories and continued throughout our childhoods. In that case, it would be pretty hard to tell a story with a beginning and a middle and an end. In that case, we would choose the model scenes, the trauma memories that would help our partner have a better felt sense of the scope, impact, and severity of our experiences. Even having those model scenes can help our partners make more sense of us, our relationships, and the moments that trauma sneaks in and puts everything in scary, slow-motion messiness.

For some trauma survivors, perhaps traumas happened in specific spaces and places, like a babysitter you had when you were six to eight years old, or specific relationships, like when I went to my grandparents' house. Perhaps, among a series of events, there are specific traumas that occurred at particular ages and stages—like puberty—that are the most devastating; these would be the stories to share.

How then, do we do it? I think we need to start with self-reflection and emotion regulation. We need to feel organized, coherent, and okay with our own stories before we share them. Start with the following exercise to clarify, for yourself, some of the secrets and how it would feel the safest to share.

Exercise: Setting the Stage for Telling the Story

Set aside an afternoon when you can put work, family, chores, and other things aside and dedicate time to self-reflection. Everyone approaches these kinds of reflections differently. If you or your partner are struggling to tolerate and make the time for this exercise, take a breath, go back to square breathing, spend some time reflecting on what is making it difficult, and start again. If you are a "dual trauma couple"—meaning that both of you have histories of trauma and you both may have disclosures to make—you will both complete both sections of this exercise: preparation for disclosure and preparation for receiving disclosure. In terms of who would disclose first, it can be as simple as flipping a coin or a game of rock–paper–scissors.

If you are still in a time of reexperiencing new memories or having flashbacks, nightmares, and intrusions of traumas that you haven't yet been able to process, integrate, and diffuse from overwhelming sensory experiences, you may want to take a lot of time to decide how to proceed. If you are working with an individual or a DCTCT therapist, it would be helpful to discuss with them whether now is the time to work on disclosures given that you are still experiencing new, vivid, and painful flashbacks and memories. However, if the decision is made to put this process on hold, that does not mean that you wouldn't pull your partner into your experience of being in a time of heightened traumatic stress. Sharing your flashbacks, nightmares, and memories is one way for you to engage in that clear signalling in the Secure Base Behaviours sequences, to get support, comfort, and care and to help your partner feel engaged and a part of your healing process.

Step One: Disclosures Begin

Sometimes all we need is a little support, structure, and safety to take the leap into sharing more about our stories and our struggles. The following exercise will take you into the process of disclosure slowly, gently, and, hopefully, safely. Remember to breathe, use your best emotion regulation skills and reach across the void into the space of co-regulation as you begin sharing more about your experiences of pain and trauma.

DISCLOSURE EXERCISE STEP ONE: DISCLOSURES BEGIN

What memories, experiences, events, and traumatic stories have you previously told your partner?

_____

_____

_____

_____

_____

_____

How much detail about what happened did you share?

_____

_____

_____

_____

_____

_____

How did your partner respond when you told them about these experiences?

_____

_____

_____

_____

_____

_____

_____

How did you experience your partner's response—thoughts, feelings, sensations, memories, embodied self-states—after sharing?

_____

_____

_____

_____

_____

_____

What memories, experiences, events, and traumatic stories has your partner shared with you?

_____

_____

_____

_____

_____

_____

How much detail did your partner share with you about their traumatic experiences?

_____

_____

_____

_____

_____

_____

_____

How did you experience your partner's sharing—thoughts, feelings, sensations, memories and stories of your own that got awakened, embodied states?

_____

_____

_____

_____

_____

_____

What impact did these disclosures have on your relationship with your partner? Did they bring you closer? Did they lead to more avoidance and isolation?

_____

_____

_____

_____

_____

_____

Did these experiences with sharing stories about your traumas, you to your partner and your partner to you, have any impact on your openness to sharing more of your story? If so, why and how? If not, why and how?

_____

_____

_____

_____

_____

_____

_____

_____

Step Two: Part One: Disclosures That Remain

Give yourself as much time to digest the responses to the first series of questions. It's okay to take a break between Step One and Step Two. This part of the exercise is designed to help you isolate and identify parts of your story you might choose to disclose next. There is no right answer. There may be experiences you aren't ready to share, for a million different reasons, and it is important to identify these and explore the *why* behind not being ready to share.

DISCLOSURE EXERCISE STEP TWO: PART ONE: DISCLOSURES THAT REMAIN

When you cast your mind back across your life, are there experiences, traumas, memories, or traumatic relationships that stand out and that you have not shared with your partner? If so, make a point form list here.

_____

_____

_____

_____

_____

_____

As you list those experiences, what comes to mind, as you reflect, about what makes it hard to share these with your partner? Do you have specific fears about what might happen? Do you have responses, emotional, bodily, thought, or others, to the idea of considering sharing these stories?

_____

_____

_____

_____

_____

_____

_____

Upon reflection, how many of those fears, feelings, or reactions do you believe are based on your own desire to avoid having to face how it would feel to share versus your fear about your partner's responses? Upon reflection are there some fears, feelings, or reactions to the idea of sharing these stories that feel like they probably wouldn't happen?

_____

_____

_____

_____

_____

_____

Make a list of the memories, experiences, stories, in order from—yeah, I could tell them that and the sky wouldn't fall—to—no way on this planet or another one am I ready to share that with my partner!

_____

_____

_____

_____

_____

_____

Now, choose one. You can do it! Choose an experience that you feel you are ready to share with your partner and write it out in as much detail as you can tolerate. Don't forget your emotion regulation skills. If you need to take breaks, do breathing exercises, or go have a dance with your partner, it's okay; take all the time that you need.

_____

_____

_____

_____

_____

_____

_____

_____

_____

_____

_____

_____

_____

_____

_____

Make a list of all of the things you fear might happen if you share this experience. As you look over the list, make a note of how you feel, in your body, as you imagine sharing the experience with your partner. Next, rank those fears on a scale of 1–10 with 1 being extremely unlikely to happen and 10 being—yup, that's totally going to happen.

_____

_____

_____

_____

_____

Take a look at the list and scan your mind and body to see how you will tolerate it if these fears do come true. Can you imagine sharing those fears with your partner? Can you imagine setting the scene with your partner to be clear about what you want and need versus what would be really hard for you, in their response?

_____

_____

_____

_____

_____

_____

Step Two: Part Two: Preparation for Partner

If you are the partner of someone who has experienced trauma, and you also have traumas of your own to share, follow the steps above in preparing for your own sharing of stories and experiences. However, there is a different preparation as a partner who will be receiving and responding to a partner's sharing of their stories of trauma and pain. So, if you have completed the above or you don't feel that you have traumas of your own to share, it will also be important to respond to these preparatory questions.

DISCLOSURE EXERCISE STEP TWO: PART TWO: PREPARATION FOR PARTNER

As the partner receiving and responding to the planned disclosure of painful experiences by your partner, what do you imagine you might feel when they share their story with you?

_____

_____

_____

_____

_____

How have you experienced disclosures in the past—from your partner or from others in your life who have entrusted you with sharing painful and traumatic stories from their life? How were those experiences for you?

_____

_____

_____

_____

_____

_____

_____

Do you have any particular thoughts, feelings, memories, sensations, or even embodied expectations, of how you might respond to your partner when they share their story with you?

_____

_____

_____

_____

_____

_____

_____

What would be helpful, for you, to share with your partner before the planned disclosure? Are there particular themes, sensory triggers, or even ways that your own trauma gets triggered that would be important to talk to your partner about before setting off on a disclosure? The goal is to share and to co-regulate in these new Secure Base Behaviour sequences—not to trigger all the trauma all over the place. So, how can your partner share what they are ready to share and how can you feel ready, regulated, and primed to receive and respond?

_____

_____

_____

_____

_____

_____

_____

Step Three: The Sharing

For the partner who is sharing first, be clear with your partner about your decision to share this experience—why is this the first? Let your partner know the Richter scale-level of the experience, in advance. Give them a sense of the pain and emotional intensity level of this experience of trauma that you are about to share so that they can prepare, as much as anyone can ever prepare for these kinds of disclosures.

It is also important, and totally okay, to set some boundaries around the sharing. Do you want your partner to hold your hand, stay quiet, ask questions throughout, or even not look at you while you are sharing? These are all okay. Boundaries that make it more comfortable for you without removing your partner's humanity, autonomy, and capacity to experience their own emotional response to what you are sharing, are very helpful to set the stage for sharing the traumatic experience.

Remember the exercises we just did to work on our Secure Base Behaviours to enhance our Earned Attachment Security? It's time for the show! Sharing your story, clearly, openly, in a fully embodied way, and with the specific goal of seeking connection, closeness, and understanding with your partner, is a very strong signal of attachment needs for connection, support, and soothing. Before you start the sharing, review those Secure Base Behaviours and the boundaries you have set, to double check that you haven't set yourselves up to fail—make sure you are clear about what you need so that your partner can receive a clear, specific, and detailed signal of your need and have parameters for response.

For instance, perhaps you've asked your partner not to look at you while you are sharing, but you then feel that your partner wasn't responding to your distress because they were looking away. Do you see where I'm going here? Set this up for success—clarity, detail, boundaries, and lots of preparatory conversations.

As an introduction to the sharing, start by giving the title and the scope of the experience—e.g. when I was eight years old, I was sexually abused by my babysitter. It went on for three years. I never told my parents.

Take a moment and check in with your partner. It is important that your partner also feels ready to receive and respond to your sharing—those vital second and third steps in the Secure Base sequence. You may want to do a co-regulation exercise together before you dive in, but certainly do a check in and make an opportunity for your partner to also share their fears about the process.

Now that you have set up the disclosure by sharing the title and scope of the experience, take your time to tell the story in as much detail as feels possible, tolerable, and within your window of emotion regulation. Being distressed and feeling all the feels is totally okay and frankly a good thing—I just want you to stay in a window of emotional experiencing that feels manageable. If you need to take a break, take a breath, or slow down, do so. Let your partner know if you would like their help to re-regulate yourself and co-regulate with them. Ask them for what you need—all of these steps are important practice as you build earned security together.

Once you have disclosed a beginning, middle, and end of your chosen first memory or experience, do a scan of yourself to see if what you shared contained all of the elements of a traumatic memory retelling—the things that you thought, that you felt, that you and others did, that you sensed and perceived, and any other vital aspects to the story that are important for you to share. If you need to add to the story, now is the time.

At this point, share with your partner how you are feeling, thinking, and sensing, and anything else that is coming up into your awareness. Ask for their support if you need help staying grounded and regulated. It will also be important to give your partner space to ask questions to clarify things they did not fully understand or take in. When you are ready, ask them to share how they are feeling, thinking, and sensing, in response to hearing about something that happened to you that was traumatic. Many partners feel anger, grief, confusion, and even shock. All of these feelings are a part of the experience and need to be shared. Take the time you need to debrief the sharing, move your bodies, walk and talk. Stay connected by holding hands or by both of you holding onto the same object, like a sweater between you, if it feels like too much or overwhelming to touch body to body.

Here are some questions from the *disclosing partner* to the *receiving partner* that you might use to talk through the experience of sharing:

- What was it like to hear about what happened to me?
- What are you thinking, feeling, sensing, imagining, now that you know about this thing that has happened to me?
- I was afraid of_____. Now that you know about this experience that I have had, is _____ something that you are—thinking—feeling—doing—sensing?
- Does knowing about this experience help you understand me and how I live our relationship more or differently?
- Does knowing about this experience change anything about how you understand our relationship and how we are together?

Does knowing about these traumatic experiences change anything about how you feel about someone— a perpetrator with whom you have ongoing contact, siblings or parent that did not protect you, etc.?

Sometimes when we share stories about abuse and traumas that we have experienced at the hands of people who should have protected and cared for us, our partners may have very strong reactions to any ongoing contact with these persons or may want to confront them. You may have been holding all of these experiences as part of your sense of who you are and what life is like for a long time. You may also have found ways to navigate the complexities of having some form of relationship with perpetrators, for all sorts of reasons, including that they are family members upon whom you might rely for some kinds of support.

For example, I maintained contact with my adoptive family because that was the only way I could have contact with the grandmother who had been so pivotal to my sense of belonging and being worthy of care. For her, the parts of me that were so problematic in my family were actually kind of great and hilarious and fun. No one else in my family thought I was anything more than a problem. I needed to stay in proximity to her until her death, and the only way to stay in contact with her was to have contact with my parents as she was living with them for the last few years of her life. After her death, I made the difficult decision to let go of contact, which also meant letting go of any fantasies I might have had of things getting better and grieving that my children would not have any extended family on my side.

When I told my partner more about my experiences and the role that my parents played in these traumas, it was very hard for her to be around them in any way. I had to accept that. However, her clarity in seeing how I was impacted by contact with my family, and her own indignance that I could have been treated in the ways that I had been treated, also helped me come to a place of acceptance about letting go.

So, your partner will have all kinds of complicated, painful, confusing, and possibly even clarifying thoughts and feelings about the people who had a role in hurting you, and that's okay. They didn't have to adapt to those relationships and those traumas for their survival. But you will have to navigate any changes that come from the disclosures that you make to one another.

Here are some questions from the *receiving partner* to the *disclosing partner* that you might use to talk through the experience of sharing:

- What was it like to tell me about what happened to you?
- What are you thinking, feeling, sensing, imagining, now that you have told me about this thing that has happened to you?
- I was afraid of _____ when you told me your story. How was it for you that I *did/did not* _____ when you told me your story?
- How can I support you in feeling okay about sharing this experience with me?
- Is there anything you need to hear from me that would help you feel secure in our relationship now that I know about this experience?

Add any other questions for one another that feel important to your own relationship and context.

When you have completed the debrief, take a break, spend some time in *parallel play*—what developmental researchers refer to as when two little people are playing nearby one another, are aware of one another, but aren't necessarily actively engaged with one another. Listen to some music, spend some time outside moving your bodies, make some kind of snack that both of you enjoy—basically, do some of the things that you do well to regroup, reground, and reorient to life.

These processes can be pretty intense and tiring. I wouldn't suggest you do this more than once a week. If you are working with a DCTCT therapist, you can use your session times to work through these disclosures in the containing space of your relationship with the therapist. If you are working on your own, find a time that you can set aside to continue to work on important sharing of the experiences that have made you both who you are. Take turns, week after week, with who will be the sharer and who will be the receiver.

If your trauma and abuse was chronic and severe, you may find that sharing model scenes of traumatic experiences is one way to share your traumas without feeling like you need to recount each experience: especially since chronic and severe trauma can blend into itself over time, moment after moment. Such a model scene could be defined as one particular episode or experience of abuse that particularly illustrates the ways in which the abuse or trauma "typically" occurred. The goal of this process is not necessarily to share the gritty, graphic, or gory details of each traumatic event but rather to fill out the story with feelings, thoughts, sensations, and relational themes. This process helps your partner understand your trauma story with as much beginning, middle, and end as you are able to share, and to help you, the trauma survivor, lift the veil of silent secrets that may have been standing between you and your partner.

Check in with the questions about setting up for disclosure, setting boundaries around sharing, and being clear about your needs. The goal is to break through any barriers that get in the way of your closeness, work through traumatic memories together, and help you feel that you can relax, be close, and not have to worry about what might "fall out" of you in moments of vulnerability.

Many years ago, I worked with an older woman who was experiencing quite severe cognitive decline and was on the verge of a diagnosis of dementia. She was terrified. She had not told her stories to the people in her life. She had built a life on the outside while also being tortured by her untold life on the inside—a swirling morass of traumatic memories and sensations that were assaulting her day and night, into her eighth decade of life. She had not told the important people in her life about her traumas, and she was terrified that it would all come tumbling out as the dementia crept further and further upon her. Her terror stuck with me, and it really reinforced how important it is to be as transparent as you can tolerate, with your partner, about the stories of pain that you carry.

Other Kinds of Secrets

Sharing our trauma stories is a vital part of breaking down barriers to closeness, building earned security in our attachment relationship, and helping our partners understand and mentalize us in ways that are more deeply embedded in our beings. Sharing our deepest pains with the person we love is one important way to draw one another closer. However, trauma stories aren't the only kind of secret that may need to be shared. There are other categories of secrets that may need to be explored, shared, processed, and even healed.

We'll talk about sexual secrets in the section on sex and sexuality but, for this section, we can talk in general about secrets we keep from our partners. Secrecy creates barriers and reinforces disconnection, in relation to how our traumas live in our everyday lives, survival strategies, and ways of coping with ongoing traumatic embodiment that feel shameful, scary, or that we feel would push our partners away from us.

In the first section of the workbook, we talked about coping strategies that might be helpful for survival but that become more of a hindrance than a help, over time. Drugs, alcohol, disordered eating, self-injury, gambling, compulsive exercise, high levels of dissociation, and many other ways of coping with overwhelming distress can really help bring floods of emotions into a tolerable range, but they can also cause harm to our bodies, minds, spirits, and relationships.

It is important to note that even within this particular category there are secrets that are simply not to be known or shared, and there are secrets that are known by both partners but are never spoken about—like a pact of silence that both agree to hold as sacred. For instance, I've worked with many trauma survivors who cope with their overwhelming feelings using alcohol or food. I would have a hard time counting the number of times that survivors, mostly women, have told me they kept their binge eating and purging or heavy alcohol consumption from their partners. At the same time, they reported living in a one bedroom, one bathroom apartment, and their partner is in the living room every night when, after dinner, they go to the bathroom and barf their guts out. In these cases it's not that the partner doesn't know what is happening: the couple has a silent, sacred pact that it will never be talked about or brought into shared knowing.

Sometimes it's hard to unravel why these secrets need to stay in the land of the unknown. Perhaps both partners benefit from the secrecy—an avoidant partner doesn't have to face the emotionality of supporting their partner in their ways of coping, and an ashamed survivor doesn't have to face the shame of their partner truly knowing how they've had to use these external strategies of drugs, alcohol, food, self-injury, and other soothing and emotion regulating behaviours, to survive. It works, but it only works to a point; it is never possible to move towards greater closeness when secrets, especially secrets about which you feel deep shame, lie between you.

JOURNAL REFLECTIONS HANDOUT: OTHER KINDS OF SECRETS

Are there other secrets you are holding away from your partner? If so, what are they?

_____

_____

_____

_____

_____

_____

Why do you feel the need to keep these secrets from your partner? What is your fear? What do you feel, think, sense, and experience inside of yourself when you think about telling your partner about this/these secrets?

_____

_____

_____

_____

_____

How do you think your partner will feel, think, sense, and experience these secrets if you were to disclose them?

_____

_____

_____

_____

_____

_____

_____

Are any of these secrets—behaviours, actions, experiences, or feelings—that you believe would be experienced as traumatic betrayals by your partner? If so, which ones and how?

_____

_____

_____

_____

_____

_____

_____

Is there one secret that feels less difficult than the others that you feel you could risk sharing?

_____

_____

_____

_____

_____

_____

_____

If you are working with a DCTCT couple therapist you may ask for, or the therapist may suggest, individual sessions for both of you. Then you have an opportunity to talk through these secrets and discuss strategies for *which*, *why*, and *when*—which secrets and for what reason and when they would be shared. Your therapist may set aside specific sessions to prepare for sharing secrets and then sessions to make disclosures. Having this support can make disclosing difficult secrets, ones that are shameful, embarrassing, or might even lead to conflict, more manageable.

If you are working without a therapist, you will not have this support to facilitate any sharing that feels important. If this is the case, look through your list and make an inventory of what secrets can be shared that will not rock the foundation of your relationship. These would be secrets that might be upsetting, confusing, of challenging for your partner to take in, such as disordered eating or alcohol and drug consumption, but that you believe your partner will be able to receive and, at least with some time to process, will move into responding with support and care.

Similar to the first category of disclosures, sharing stories of pain and trauma, it is important to set aside specific times for sharing and to prepare. Letting our partners know that we are going to share some parts of our selves and our lives—that they don't know about and that might be upsetting—is a part of the preparation. This allows our partners to come to the discussion knowing that emotion regulation and co-regulation may be an important skill to keep online.

I have certainly sat with couples where these kinds of secrets come out, and they can cause some upheaval. A partner that is not aware of their partner's substance use difficulties can feel confused, surprised, alienated, angry, and even humiliated. These feelings need space, and so we have to hold our mentalizing and emotion-regulation capacities in hand to allow that space and time. That kind of secret may not have started to spill into the relationship.

I have also worked with couples where one partner has engaged in some risky and dangerous gambling or spending behaviours, and these have depleted savings or even put the couple in a financially precarious situation. Partners hearing about these kinds of secrets can also be very surprised, confused, afraid, and angry, and experience all manner of feelings, thoughts, sensations and even triggers to their own traumas. Everyone needs the time to breathe, reflect, process. and come together to support the trauma survivor partner in making necessary changes to protect their body, spirit, and the relationship—including the financial stability of the home and family.

I would encourage you to seek out the support of a DCTCT or trauma-informed couple therapist to help you through any disclosures of secrets that feel more likely to cause earthquake action in your relationship. Therapists with these areas of expertise can be hard to find, but if you are able to seek out this kind of support it would be very helpful. When navigating disclosures that might lead a partner to feel blindsided, confused, disoriented, or even betrayed, it would be really helpful to have the guiding hand of a good couple therapist.

Trauma Processing in a Dyadic Context

At this stage of DCTCT, if you were working with a therapist who was following the treatment manual it would be time to start working to process some of your traumatic experiences. The therapist would guide you through this and this workbook would support you in preparing for, going through, and then debriefing processing sessions. If you are not working with a therapist, you'll need to give thought to what memories are important for you to work through with your partner, and which memories you have the capacity and tolerance to work through without a therapist.

We will be working with triggers that arise in your relationship that are linked to traumatic memories. The focus of this particular trauma-processing exercise is to contain the ways in which memories of past traumas get triggered and come alive in your relationship. This can mean that we work directly with a specific traumatic experience, but more often it means working directly with the triggers, to help you identify why and how the triggers arise and then assign them back to the old trauma rather than the new relationship.

I will try to guide you through the process of deciding how deep to go into the trauma trigger exploration and the memories that are attached. Still, you will need to trust your instincts on this one, as there is no way to know with certainty which memories can be worked through with a partner without too much intolerable distress, and without retraumatizing you and your partner.

The goal of trauma processing, in general, is to shift the experience of the trauma from a present reliving to a past memory, a part your life story. Traumas cannot be memories until they no longer affect us as if they are still happening right now. We carry those imprints on our entire beings—body, mind, self, and spirit. It's as though our bodies, minds, and sensation selves are living in fear for something that has already happened—we are poised for trauma, but the trauma happened; it's over, but we can't let it be in the past because it's on a loop inside of us, going on over and over and over again.

The goal of DCTCT is not to transform these memories somehow into painless or unimportant parts of your history; these traumatic experiences will always be "bad" memories. You will always carry the story of pain, but I want you to carry it in a bag that says: really bad things that have happened in the past, but they are no longer happening in the present. These memories can become a part your story—sad and painful, to be certain, but no longer deeply embedded and embodied, no longer living as in the

DOI: 10.4324/9781003330950-22

present moment. How amazing would it be to no longer live in fear of trauma popping out without advance notice, sucking us into the past pretending to be the present, sweeping us away from the life we are trying to build and into a past that needs to be put back in its place.

It's important here to remind ourselves that some traumas are not in the past and we have to respect those differences. If there continues to be violence in your relationship, it may not be the time to put hypervigilance into its place in the story of the past. If you are a racialized, trans/non-binary, or indigenous person, you are living racism, transphobia, and the impacts of colonialism every day. It's very hard to distinguish, in our bodies, the difference between past traumas that can be mapped into our personal stories of life and pain from the ways we still need to be on guard to protect ourselves from very real threats that exist in the world to people living daily oppression, dealing with housing and food insecurity, job instability, racism, homophobia, transphobia, xenophobia, antisemitism, and colonialism.

In this section of the workbook, we seek to find ways to work through some memories that you feel are impinging on your ability to feel safe, close, connected, and secure with your partner. And, in fact, when the past really does live in the past, it can give us more resources, emotionally, relationally, and even physiologically, to address the traumas that continue in our present. I don't think I even noticed experiences of homophobia in my life until I did a lot of trauma-processing work. In my own being, life was dangerous everywhere, in all places, in all relationships, so homophobia was just one more place of danger. Being in a different state of being around my own traumas has allowed me to notice more clearly if I am actually in danger, because the past is living where it belongs: in the past.

Trauma processing with a partner unfolds seamlessly from the process of disclosure we just worked through; these are not separate processes. As the stories are told, the thoughts, feelings, triggers, and rough patches that may previously have been avoided are laid bare. Healing begins through the experience of telling the story. As we tell our stories to our partners, we may become even more aware than we were before of how much certain parts of traumatic experiences and relationships are crowding out our current relationship with our partner.

This workbook is supporting you to explore traumas that occurred in the past, mostly during important periods of development such as childhood. The focus is not on shared traumas, such as when a couple experiences a devastating loss, or an accident, or a stillbirth. Where traumas are shared, the process shifts from one where one partner is sharing, and another is supporting, to one where both partners are processing the same trauma but each from their own unique vantage point. These are also very important to work through and to seek out as much support as you need, to be able to get to a place of clarity, regulation, co-regulation, closeness, and coherence. When you are taking turns sharing traumatic material, it is a lot easier for you, as a couple, to hold onto your regulation and mentalizing because one of you can work hard to stay on dry land, emotionally. For these shared traumas it is much more difficult, as you are both in the trauma at the same time. For these, I would really recommend seeking out a DCTCT therapist or someone informed in trauma who works with couples.

There are many different approaches to trauma processing, and they differ from one another. When working with a therapist, you will have a different experience of processing based on the training and theories that a therapist has been exposed to. Approaches will also differ as a result of the nature of the traumas you may have experienced, the age you were when the traumas occurred, and many other factors. All of these processes have one underlying goal, to help you transform traumatic memories held as sensory, somatic, emotional, and cognitive time capsules—locked away in the body as if they were living in the present tense and experienced as still happening when they emerge in response to triggers or reminders of the original event.

Most approaches to trauma processing are based on something called "exposure", which in essence means exposing yourself to the memory in a different way, to allow the charge to be diffused from it. These interventions focus on helping trauma survivors recount traumatic experiences in detail, without avoiding emotions and sensations, until the experiences are no longer emotionally overwhelming. However, many trauma survivors find it very difficult to tolerate the intensity of these approaches without first developing skills in emotion regulation; exposure-based interventions can cause severe emotional flooding, feeling like we're being pulled back in time and not being able to manage in our daily lives. This is one of the big reasons we start our work by building up emotion regulation and mentalizing skills before diving in. We can proceed after working to build a secure base with our partner through practising security-based strategies to meet their attachment needs, which tends to protect the survivor from being completely overwhelmed or retraumatized.

Bringing your partner into the experience of traumatic memory processing gives us an added support in facing painful memories and feelings; this can help us to persevere with the trauma work when it starts to feel too painful and maybe impossible. Engaging in trauma processing with your partner also includes your partner in the experience of healing and gives you, as a couple, new experiences of safety and closeness as well as new opportunities to practise building a Secure Base. The goal here is to help you, the trauma survivor, *both* to resolve trauma symptoms *and* to improve intimacy, closeness, self and co-regulation, and overall relationship satisfaction.

At the beginning of the workbook, we explored trauma triggers from a few angles, such as psychoeducation, emotion regulation, and building attachment security during times of emotional distress. Overall, however, the emphasis has always come back to helping you and your partner to identify, communicate, and develop strategies to manage the trigger itself. We haven't yet begun to look at processing the traumas that are fuelling those triggers and bring you back into states of reliving and flashbacks.

One acronym that some trauma therapists use to help clients understand how traumatic experiences get stuck in our beings and don't move on through and get stored into our autobiographical memory is *BASK—Behaviour, Affect, Sensation,* and *Knowledge.* This acronym identifies the aspects of a memory that can get stuck in us when traumas have happened to us and how we need to explore each aspect of the memory to dislodge them from their stuck place and turn them into painful but not stuck memories. The B—Behaviour—represents the things you might have done during a traumatic experience: did you run, hide, hurt yourself, hurt someone else? The A—Affect—represents what you felt emotionally at the time: were you afraid, shut down, ashamed, etc.? The S—Sensation—refers to what sensations you might have felt in your body—did you feel dizzy, nauseated, pain? What might you have seen, felt, smelled, heard, in your sensory self? And K—Knowledge—refers to what you know about the traumatic experience, the who, why, where, when, and the what. You might also know things like the context that led up to the event or factors that might be conspiring to raise the temperature in the household and raise the risk for violence.

Each of those aspects of memory can be "smooshed" together in weird ways; it can get stuck in your body or mind and come howling out when a related trigger is activated. For instance, imagine having been sexually abused as a young child. Many young children don't know what sex is, so things are happening to their bodies that are excruciatingly painful, and possibly confusingly pleasurable, but there is no K—Knowledge about what is happening so, all of the physicality gets linked to S—Sensation and A—Affect. And then, perhaps the sexual abuse occurred in your bedroom, but in the dark, and your abuser put a pillow over your head so you didn't know who was hurting you. Then, you don't have the S—Sensation of sight and seeing who was abusing you and the K—Knowledge of this being your grandfather that you loved and who behaved completely differently during the day. In this case, the Knowledge is missing, but there are still the Sensations of how that person smelled, felt against your skin, and the sound of their noises and utterances.

The BASK elements of this traumatic memory link emotions to body sensations, sensations linked to what should be but isn't knowledge, and other elements of memory that have become uncoupled from a normal autobiographical memory. A typical autobiographical memory would be a memory with a beginning, middle, and end, words that can describe the events with all of the BASK elements linked to the "right" part of the memory.

Another way traumatic experiences become unlinked from typical autobiographical memories is when a trauma occurs while someone isn't conscious. That could mean the person had been drugged and was not conscious, but violence was happening to their body, or they were an infant who did not yet have any way to "symbolize", to put language and consciousness to an event, or even if someone had experienced such severe trauma that they dissociated to such a degree that they were not conscious of what was happening to them. In these situations, traumatic events get very deeply stuck into the body and emotional channels of memory, and so the only way that those experiences are expressed is through emotional flashbacks or sensory flashbacks called body memories.

Our goal then is to integrate all of the bits and pieces of the memories into one coherent and complete memory that has a beginning, middle, and end, and all of the elements of BASK. For some experiences that will never be possible: such as those that happen during infancy or early childhood when there is no language or consciousness of the kind that makes memory stories. Even for these, however, we do what we can to integrate the aspects of memory that can be felt, sensed, known, and experienced in the mind and body, back into a story of the past and out of the linkages that are triggering it in the present.

The next exercise goes back to explore the triggers you have identified as intruding into your relational life, what traumatic memories, sensations, and feelings become relived in ways that impact your couple relationship.

JOURNAL REFLECTIONS HANDOUT: TRAUMATIC MEMORIES AND YOUR RELATIONSHIP

What sensory triggers pull you back into traumatic memories? How do these arise in your relationship?

_____

_____

_____

_____

_____

_____

_____

Are you conscious of the BASK of those traumatic memories and do you have a sense of why these come up in your relationship?

_____

_____

_____

_____

_____

_____

_____

What happens to time/feelings/your body when you have a flashback? Are you able to turn to your partner to help them understand what is happening to you? Are you able to seek comfort and support when you experience traumatic memories resurfacing?

_____

_____

_____

_____

_____

_____

_____

Are there particular things that your partner may do or say that can trigger you? Are there particular ways that your partner might speak/touch/respond to you that trigger you?

_____

_____

_____

_____

_____

_____

When you are having a flashback, are you aware of what is happening around you?

_____

_____

_____

_____

_____

_____

If your partner tries to speak/touch/hold you during a flashback, what is that like for you?

_____

_____

_____

_____

_____

_____

When you are triggered, what helps you get grounded and re-regulated? Are you able to co-regulate with your partner when you are triggered? If so, how? If not, what makes that hard?

_____

_____

_____

_____

_____

_____

_____

Are there particular things that your partner does/says that you find very helpful or very unhelpful when you are triggered?

_____

_____

_____

_____

_____

_____

_____

Traumatic Memory Processing

If you are a dual trauma couple, both of you will do this journalling reflection exercise, independently. Once you have had a chance to review, reflect, and re-regulate yourself in responding to these journal prompts, it will be time to share these reflections with your partner, if you feel that you are both ready and can hold onto your emotion regulation and mentalizing capacities.

Make sure to set aside time to explore these reflections with your partner. It can be difficult for our partners to hear that their attempts to soothe and care for us when we are in distress can be experienced as unhelpful, dysregulating, and even a trigger for flashbacks and other traumatic memories. Go slow, and try to notice ways in which your partner is able to be helpful, soothing, reorienting, or comforting. Remember, the traumas that you are reliving in those triggered moments are something you and your partner can fight together.

EXERCISE: LIST OF TRIGGERS HANDOUT

Make a short-form list of the ways in which you experience traumatic memories coming alive in your relationship. This can include triggers directly related to the behaviours, emotions, and traumas of your partner, as well as things that are outside of your relationship but come into the relationship in some way.

_____

_____

_____

_____

_____

_____

_____

Sharing

Once each of you has developed a full list of triggers, take the time to share them with one another, and provide as much context as you can tolerate. All of these exercises involve turn taking and making sure that adequate time is set aside for each partner. Given how challenging and painful these memories and triggers can be, you may want to space out these sessions of sharing, at least enough that you both can really get re-regulated and co-regulated back together.

In the following example, the trauma survivor shares the trigger: the thing that happens to activate the traumatic memory, then shares their response: in this case mostly S—Sensations—and B—Behaviours—feeling panic, terror, embodiment of the terror, and the desire to run.

When you get upset with me for falling asleep with our daughter after telling her a story at bedtime, I start to feel panicky, and my body goes cold and shivery and my stomach starts to hurt and all I can feel is terror and I want to run away. I think that that is because my father used to get very angry with me if I tried to go to bed with my sisters to avoid him coming into my bed at night to sexually abuse me. I know this in my head, but my body can't separate you and my father in those moments.

It can be very hard to stay regulated and grounded, when sharing these kinds of experiences of how the past intrudes on the present in our relationships. Try to share both the trigger and as much awareness as you can find about how the past is intruding on the present. Include any whisper of awareness you have that it isn't the actual feelings of your partner in that moment that are leading you to that distress but, rather, how those feelings become linked to an old and incompletely processed traumatic memory.

Journal Reflections: For Partners

JOURNAL REFLECTIONS HANDOUT: FOR PARTNERS

For partners, this is an important moment to listen, regulate, reflect, and respond. Can you take in the ways in which your partner is sharing that they "know" about the difference between the past and the present, but they can't unlink the two?

_____

_____

_____

_____

_____

_____

_____

Can you sit and listen without getting pulled into defensiveness or anger?

_____

_____

_____

_____

_____

_____

Can you hold onto your mentalizing and emotion regulation and also pry the past away from the present?

_____

_____

_____

_____

_____

_____

_____

Are there any traumatic triggers that get activated in response to your partner's sharing of their triggers?

_____

_____

_____

_____

_____

_____

_____

Making a List Together

Once you have had the time to reflect and review, share your responses to these journal prompts with your partner.

I'm sure this feels a bit stilted, slow, and artificial but these are really challenging traumatic experiences that are getting activated in day-to-day life. This means they are still hot to the touch, and we need to be careful and thoughtful, and go slow. Given that you will probably need to share a number of triggers to traumatic memories with one another, and then reflect and respond, take turns being the sharer and the responder and take as long as it takes to go through your lists.

In this next step, the two of you can work together to develop another list of possible ways to work with the triggers you have identified, shared, and reflected upon. The goal of this process is to reduce distress, re-experiencing, and emotional dysregulation in response to reminders of the traumas and triggers that happen in your relationship; it will not necessarily make the triggers vanish completely. As you make your list, focus on the strategies that would help you notice the little space of reflection between the past and present when you get triggered; try to create an antidote to the trauma by turning towards one another, providing comfort, and working through the trigger directly rather than avoiding it.

For most triggers, being able to talk it through, to share the BASK elements that have become linked with something happening in the relationship, and to move towards one another with support, is the best response we can hope for. If we do want these triggers and the responses, where the past intrudes on your present relationship, to gradually diminish—exposure in the form of direct sharing of the memory is one important way to make that happen. Making the link to the present in the form of a trigger and turning towards one another for comfort and support: these can be important parts of the work towards a behavioural change.

For instance, one of you might be particularly triggered when you are standing at the sink, doing dishes, and your partner comes up behind you to bring you the remainder of the dishes from the dining room table. Perhaps the sound of the feet approaching reminds you of your father approaching you from behind in the lead-up to brutal sexual abuse. Or maybe it is that when you cannot see someone coming, you become startled and afraid but cannot quite put your finger on why this is a trigger.

EXERCISE: MAKING A LIST TOGETHER HANDOUT

What is one thing that the two of you could do to signal to one another that you are in the present and not in the traumatizing past when a trigger gets activated?

_____

_____

_____

_____

_____

_____

What kind of strategy might be helpful to manage situations where one of you gets startled and triggered into an old memory? Examples could include agreeing to say something to each other when entering a room or when approaching your partner from behind. Come up with something that will work for your relationship.

_____

_____

_____

_____

_____

_____

Do the two of you have lock and key triggers that make it hard for one of you to keep your feet on dry land? If so, what are these and why is it so hard to pull yourself out of it? For instance: one of you might be very triggered by the sound of someone walking in socked feet across the floor on the floor above them. Meanwhile, the other may get very triggered by the idea of wearing shoes in the house having been physically abused for running into the house with shoes on because they were playing outside and didn't notice that they had to go to the bathroom and by the time they did notice, they didn't have time to take their shoes off. What are your triggers that are like this?

_____

_____

_____

_____

_____

_____

For lock and key triggers, can you develop a strategy that one of you can hold onto in the present and signal to the other (that you both agree upon is the sign) that you aren't living in a trauma-tizing moment, that you are with each other, that you can pull yourselves out of the spiral of those embedded triggers. What might your strategy look like? Sometimes the funnier or sillier the better—nothing like laughter to pull us back into relationship and back into our bodies.

_____

_____

_____

_____

_____

_____

Hold onto one another and all of your newfound capacities to regulate, mentalize, and connect to one another. As you find your way back to one another and explore how to build these new responses and ways of being with one another that are more attuned, clear, relational, and unglued from the traumas of the past, you will slowly find yourself in a new relational world, a relational world of gentleness, compassion, and, the shared ability to find your way out of these hard places of repetition and pain.

Journal Reflections: How Are We Changing?

Once you have been about to explore your relational triggers in depth, together, you can begin to explore how your relationship is changing in response to a greater understanding of each other's histories and traumas. Many of you will have already had a lot of individual psychotherapy before starting on the journey of healing your relationship. However, that doesn't mean that the process of sharing your trauma stories and triggers, and your awareness of how you are living trauma in the present, will be easy. You may find that you have more flashbacks, more intrusions into your daily life, and more thoughts, feelings, sensations, and impulses, when your traumatic experiences intrude into your relationship. This is to be expected and makes sense—you are poking a big bucket of bears, so the bears are going to have something to say about that. However, through this intentional process, this state should be temporary. If it is not temporary, and if you find yourself being swallowed up by traumatic memories you felt you had settled and worked through, seek out a DCTCT therapist or a trauma-informed couple therapist to help you integrate all that you have shared. You may, however, find that you are more able to turn to your partner for support as you go through this temporary upsurge of traumatic distress. You may also find that your partner is more able to respond, as you are both learning to share in different ways that enhance the growing earned security between you.

JOURNAL REFLECTIONS HANDOUT: HOW ARE WE CHANGING?

What are you noticing about how you get triggered, respond to triggers, and experience being activated by present life awakening past traumatic memories, that may be changing as you work through these exercises with your partner?

_____

_____

_____

_____

_____

_____

_____

What are you noticing about how your partner responds to you, when you are triggered, that may be changing as you work through these exercises?

_____

_____

_____

_____

_____

_____

What are you noticing about how you respond to your partner, when they are triggered, that may be changing as you work through these exercises?

_____

_____

_____

_____

_____

_____

Think about making these disconnected pieces into a complete autobiographical narrative that has a beginning, middle, end, and links the BASK elements to their "correct" part of the memory. When you reflect on the triggers that you have been exploring with your partner, do you notice any change in how the BASK elements of those memories are connected or, not connected, to the whole story?

_____

_____

_____

_____

_____

_____

Which triggers, from your original list, do you feel you need to do more work on with your partner? What do you notice about these triggers that is different from the ones that you feel more resolved and settled about?

_____

_____

_____

_____

_____

_____

As you reflect on your progress from writing out your list of triggers to sharing them with your partner, and then working through them step by step, what do you notice about your sense of connection, security, closeness, and co-regulation, with your partner? If there are positive changes, how do you understand these and what is it like to feel these positive changes? If there are some things that feel more activated or difficult since you started this process, how do you understand this and are there ways that you and your partner might continue in this work to help them settle and reconnect?

_____

_____

_____

_____

_____

_____

As you continue to work through the workbook, you may come back to this section over and over again to look at those triggers with fresh eyes, to continue to explore the ways in which the past infiltrates your present relationship when you get triggered into old traumatic memories by things happening in the present. That is okay: therapists like to talk about these processes as a lot like peeling an onion. You may take off a layer of the onion but there are more layers underneath. Each layer will add richness and depth to the work you are doing and, hopefully, help you and your partner continue towards building that earned security and great closeness and connection.

Sex and Sexuality

For many of you, conflicts and challenges around sex are front and centre when you think about your relationship and how trauma is impacting your couple life. For others, sex and sexuality are in the background; you are more concerned about resolving conflicts, finding ways to feel more connected in daily life, and building Earned Secure attachment. Many of the couples I work with haven't had sex in years. Some are even surprised that I ask them about their sexual relationship, as though it's absurd that anyone in so much distress could possibly be worrying about sex. For others, despite all of their daily distress, triggers, and conflict, sex is the way that they are able to feel close to one another and resolve feelings of alienation and distress: so they guard it preciously. The following section is specifically about sex and sexual healing for yourself and your partner. If you don't feel ready to dive in there, take your time, and go as slowly as you need to stay regulated and grounded. It's also okay if the topic of sexual healing is not yet on your agenda. The workbook isn't going anywhere, and you can come back to it any time you feel ready and interested.

Conflicts around sex rarely arise, primarily, out of aspects like where, when, why, and how—it's not whether we have sex at a set time on Sunday morning or whether we do the horizontal tango in the living room; it's all about compatibility and cohesion. If both partners are perfectly content having sex once a year on one of your birthdays, that's just fine. But, if one of you wants to have sex once a year and the other of wants to have sex five times a day, you know you have struggle and conflict in your future. The same goes for the what of sex—if one of you feels curious about using sex toys or dressing up and role playing, and the other of you finds those things triggering or distasteful, that's where you have trouble. It isn't about what you get up to sexually, it's how compatible you and your partner are in terms of desires, fantasies, frequency, and intensity.

That said, there are some very particular struggles that trauma survivors may experience in their sexual relationships, their sense of themselves as sexual beings, and their connection to the embodiment and vulnerability that sex can arouse.

At one time, "experts" believed that only sexual abuse survivors would have challenges with sex. Now we understand that any kind of trauma, especially in childhood and perpetrated by an adult who should have been a carer and protector, can lead to sexual difficulties. If you think about it, that makes sense. While sexual abuse survivors can have very specific triggers and vulnerabilities around sex, all interpersonal trauma survivors have had the experience of being hurt and betrayed by someone who should have taken

DOI: 10.4324/9781003330950-23

care of them and who they should have been able to trust. This, by itself, can be enough to interfere with letting down your guard, allowing yourself to enter your body, to be open to sexual stimulation, and to be vulnerable with a partner in the ways that can make sex really great.

Culture, Family, and Sex for Survivors

Speaking directly and with plain language about sex and sexuality can be hard, especially for those who grew up in families and cultures where sex was not discussed openly. However, it is important to find a way through, so that this important part of your relationship isn't left to fester in a closet because you don't have the language or comfort to talk about it. In my work I have found that couples very quickly engage with talking about their sexual thoughts, feelings, and experiences when given permission by me, their therapist. If you are working on your own through the workbook—just give each other permission.

  It's okay to laugh here. When I was about twelve, my mother sat me down with a big encyclopaedia open to a page with lovely illustrations of genitals on it. She went through "the talk" like a robot, telling me about what body parts went where and how this was sex and sex is where babies came from. That I was already under assault by my father, her sexual partner, did not lessen the irony for me, but she was pretty committed in her desire to do her duty. To me, it sounded awful. No doubt something about how she told me the details communicated a bit of distaste and disgust, but I asked her "why would anyone want to do that?" This was a legitimate question—I really could *not* imagine ever wanting to do *that*! Her response was, "some people like it". Oof. That is the only conversation that was ever had on this topic in my WASP (white Anglo-Saxon protestant) household. I tell you this story, which at the time was horrifying and traumatizing but that I now find hilarious, to illustrate how much our cultural and familial backgrounds and traditions play into how we feel about sex, how we talk about sex, and how we navigate getting our needs met and our pleasures known. For me, my family culture matched the culture in which I was raised. This can become even more challenging, painful, confusing, and messy when our family cultures, racial or ethnic, religious or language identities, do not "match" the majority culture.

JOURNAL REFLECTIONS HANDOUT: FAMILY, CULTURE, AND SEX

How was sex talked about in your family? What were the messages you took away from that?

_____

_____

_____

_____

_____

_____

_____

If you are a sexual abuse survivor, was there a disconnect between how sex was talked about in your family and how the abuse was perpetrated? For instance, the story above with my mother being so overtly disgusted by the idea of sex while my father continued to be a sexual predator towards me. Or, being in a family where people talk about sex openly and with laughter but, then, sexual abuse is perpetrated in ways that promote shame, self-hatred, and are painful and destructive.

_____

_____

_____

_____

_____

_____

How is sex represented in your culture? How was sex talked about? What were the attitudes? Did mutuality, vulnerability, pleasure, and consent get talked about? What are the messages that you take away from this?

_____

_____

_____

_____

_____

What kinds of gender differences are there around sex in your family and culture? Did these play a role, at all, in your trauma experiences? What messages did you take away from them?

_____

_____

_____

_____

_____

_____

_____

If you are trans or non-binary, how did you navigate those gender differences around sex as you grew up? Were you able to come out and feel safe and accepted by your family and community and grow into a sexual self? If you were not, what was this like for you to navigate and how did you handle becoming embodied in your gender identity while also growing into a sexual person? How did your trauma intersect with these areas of your development?

_____

_____

_____

_____

_____

_____

_____

Were there conflicts that you experienced between your culture and family's attitudes and values around sex and sexuality and that of adjacent cultures? Did these play a role in how your trauma unfolded? Did racism, and other forms of oppression play a role in any sexual trauma that you experienced? If so, how did this happen and what did you take away from those experiences in terms of your own feelings, values, and attitudes about sex?

_____

_____

_____

_____

_____

_____

_____

Are you and your partner able to share these thoughts, beliefs, feelings, values, and attitudes about sex, openly with one another?

_____

_____

_____

_____

_____

_____

Have you and your partner been able to talk openly about sexual triggers, how these intersect with culture and family, and how they now impact your sexual relationship? If so, how? If not, what is making that hard?

_____

_____

_____

_____

_____

_____

_____

Our Traumatized, Embodied, Sexual Selves

For many of us, the impacts of sexual trauma become embedded in our bodies, our sense of ourselves, and our relational openness to physical, sensual, and sexual connection. When we start to explore these impacts in greater depth it can be tricky, because we can fall into assumptions about what is "right" or "normal" in relation to our bodies and our sexual selves. This can be quite hurtful and damaging.

For many trauma survivors, especially those who have experienced sexual abuse, our bodies become battlegrounds for pain, disconnection, dysregulation, disgust, and self-hatred. It is as though what was *done to* us has *become* us. It is very hard to shake this since sex and sexuality are such embodied aspects of our self and our self in relationships. Reconnecting, reconciling, forgiving, and embracing our traumatized bodies is one of the biggest hurdles to moving forward sexually. Making peace with our bodies, allowing pleasure to be welcome and tolerable. and moving away from pleasure as a shameful reminder of trauma, while learning to feel able to be expansive, expressive, and excited in our bodies, can be such a challenge.

Adding the complexities of being trans or non-binary and living with feelings of dysmorphia and dysphoria—on top of the conflicts related to trauma and, in some ways, magnified by them—can make this process of healing our sexual selves even more challenging. And then, all of the ways in which survivors may turn inwards and attack our bodies in a desperate attempt to stay regulated and sane in the aftermath of trauma also adds to this complicated struggle towards healing. Many survivors have physical scars from self-injury, stretch marks from messed up eating behaviours, and other marks of the ways in which we use our bodies as battlegrounds for our survival. And, of course, so many of us have the scars of the trauma itself—the fibroids and endometriosis of an over-traumatized uterus and abdominal cavity, scarring on vaginas and rectums from violent penetration of objects and penises at tender ages, far before little bodies were developed for even loving, consensual, pleasurable sex.

In a recent research project where we were asking trans and non-binary trauma survivors about their sexual healing journeys, many of the survivors talked about disability as a major impediment to their sexualities. These disabilities related to all of the ways that trauma lives on in our bodies, both directly (scarring, injuries, broken and damaged bodies) and indirectly (hyperactive immune systems resulting in high levels of autoimmune disorders and arthritis, early and damaging trauma to sexual organs leading to immunological responses to cause reproductive health issues, and other issues like irritable bowel disorder and Crohn's caused by all of the stress and reactivity of a survivor's body just trying to survive the unsurvivable). The list really does go on and on. How can we gentle ourselves into a little less self-hatred and a little more comfort and ease?

JOURNAL REFLECTIONS HANDOUT: OUR RELATIONSHIP WITH OUR BODY

When you think about your body, what are the first three words that come to mind?

_____

_____

_____

_____

_____

_____

_____

When you feel your way into your body, letting yourself notice the sensations, pain, comfort, nothingness, anythingness, what do you find?

_____

_____

_____

_____

_____

_____

When you think about sex, what are the first three words that come to mind?

_____

_____

_____

_____

_____

Have you had pleasurable sexual experiences that have felt fully embodied, luscious, sensual, and beautiful? If so, can you describe the main characteristics of these?

_____

_____

_____

_____

_____

_____

Are there ways in which your relationship with your body gets in the way of being able to be embodied, feel your sexuality and sensuality, and allow sexual arousal and pleasure?

_____

_____

_____

_____

_____

_____

Are you able to pleasure yourself through masturbation to orgasm, with or without toys? Does this feel okay, good, yummy, or yucky, scary, and retraumatizing?

_____

_____

_____

_____

_____

_____

When your partner moves towards you, sexually, are you able to tell, or show them, what would bring you pleasure? Can you be open and allow them to be with you in ways that bring you to an orgasm that feels great at the level of sensation and relationship? If so, is this something that you have learned and worked on over time with your partner or, have you always felt able to meet a partner in that way? If not, what are the barriers—thoughts, feelings, sensations, memories, and even numb empty spaces—that might be playing a role in finding this hard?

_____

_____

_____

_____

_____

_____

If your partner struggles to feel comfortable with you, sexually and sensually, what is that like for you and your relationship with your body and sexuality? How do you feel? What do you think? How does it impact your sexuality and sexual wellbeing?

_____

_____

_____

_____

_____

_____

What else comes to mind and body when you allow yourself to reflect on your relationship with your body, your sexual body, and your openness to sensuality and sex?

_____

_____

_____

_____

_____

_____

It's All About Consent and Communication

I have worked with many couples where one or both partners identified as asexual, meaning that they do not feel like one of the main ways that they engage with a partner (or partners) is through sex and sexuality. When only one partner identifies as asexual, in a couple where things are working well, what was navigated between the couple was how to meet the sexual needs of the more sexually-interested partner without impinging on the partner that identifies as asexual. Can we say that there is a direct relationship between someone experiencing trauma and then identifying as asexual? No, we can't.

There are many ways of experiencing our embodied selves. Similarly, there are many who feel that any form of pain, control, or domination, in sexual activities such as BDSM (Bondage, Domination, Sado-Masochism) reflect ways that we have been "damaged" by sexual trauma, and that we are just reliving and reexperiencing our traumas over and over again. But then there are just as many folks who would argue that BDSM is a way of reclaiming their sexuality and sexual selves from the control, pain, and domination of perpetrators. For many, the dividing line between any form of sexual engagement being okay or not okay is around consent, compulsivity, and concrete repetitions. So, if there is anyone not consenting, if the sex is compulsive, and if the sex is a concrete repetition of trauma, this is where many of us therapists feel some concern and want to explore more about what's happening. The only thing I really know is that we need to respect that we are all looking to live the fullest lives we are able, to heal as much as is possible, and to be respected and cared for in ways that feel good.

When our values, beliefs, desires, and passions conflict with those of our partners, it's part of the process of building security and closeness to be able to talk it through and work it out. For some couples, that means finding ways for one partner to be sexual while the other looks on, holds them, or even watches pornography with them. For other couples that might mean moving towards forms of consensual, ethical non-monogamy or polyamory, to give space for one partner to explore aspects of their sexuality that don't fit with the needs, desires, values, and passions of the other. There are good resources for navigating non-monogamy and polyamory, and I would encourage you to seek them out should you be feeling like that might be one way for you and your partner to manage sexualities and sexual selves that don't quite mesh and that don't seem to be coming towards cohesion. What matters is consent and communication—there is no right way to be an embodied sexual or asexual being, but it is important that if we are in relationship with others that we respect their attachment needs, sexual needs, and relational safety.

As They Say—You've Got to Love Yourself First!

You may have completed the journalling reflections on your relationship with your body and sexuality and identified that you have not found ways to feel pleasure, arousal, and orgasm, through masturbation or other self-pleasuring activities. If so, it would be important to take that on as a project. It really is hard to communicate to a partner what you want and need, sexually, if you don't know.

There are resources out there for survivors of trauma in relation to their sexual selves and sexual healing. I will admit to not loving what's out there: they are either too fluffy bunny and patronizing or they are super graphic in ways that are fine if they are fine but if you aren't ready for that level of graphic, it may be too late once you open that door. What I would suggest is to set aside time to work through the following steps, moving towards becoming more comfortable with your body, sexual stimulation, sexual arousal, orgasm, and do so over and over again until you feel you're a pro and can start helping your partner by showing them what works for you and your healing body.

Exercise: Finding Your Way to Your Own Sexual Body (See the Exercise Handout at the end of the steps)

Step One: Mental Body Scan

The first step is probably the hardest so make time, make space, turn off your phone and your computer, tell your partner that you are working on this exercise and that you need some time to yourself and, if you have kids at home, ask your partner to truck them off to the park for some wholesome playtime in nature.

When you feel ready, and you have your list of regulating activities that work for you, nearby, find your way into a space or place in which you usually feel comfortable. That can be the bed, the bathtub, the couch, a room with a lock on the door: whatever works for you to feel safe and comfortable, as comfortable as you are able. Once you have found your spot, put yourself in whatever clothing—or no clothing—you feel the most comfortable. If you are most comfortable in sweats, that's just fine; pyjamas—no problem; naked as the day you were born—all good; whatever you feel safe and comfortable in is okay. Check that the temperature in your room and your body is regulated to what allows you the most openness.

Once you've found yourself in the most comfortable space, clothing, and temperature, and have settled in, just do a body scan—noticing, from toes up or head down, what you are feeling in your body. What are you sensing, noticing, and thinking, and how does that change from moment to moment? Do you feel any sensations? Do you know how to notice a sexual or sensual sensation? What happens inside you when you do notice a sensual or sexual sensation? If you start to feel triggered or activated, are you able to breathe yourself back into a safe zone? Just noticing, tracking, sensing, and being, that is your first step.

Step Two: Felt Body Scan

Once you have completed Step One as many times as would allow you to feel calm, comfortable, at ease in your body and space, and you are able to re-regulate yourself if you feel triggered or activated, it's time to move on to Step Two. Step Two involves all of the steps of Step One while adding to the body scan. In Step One you did a mental body scan to notice the feelings, sensations, thoughts, impulses, and memories that arouse and swirl around with just being with your body. In Step Two, I want you to start with the mental body scan and then add a felt body scan. You can start at the toes or the head, hands or hips, whatever makes the most sense to how you understand your body, and just slowly move your hands across your whole body including your breasts, genitals or any other erogenous zones that feel connected to your sexual and sensual self. Notice sensations, thoughts that emerge, memories that pop up, activation and triggers that might be trying to pull you back into old traumas, and any sensual or sexual thoughts, feelings, sensations, or bodily responses like lubrication, erection of nipples or scrotum and penis, tautness in your body and even awareness of impulses to move into sexual activity with yourself. If there are parts of your body that you really can't tolerate sensing, touching, feeling, or knowing, that's okay, just take notice and make sure to reflect on that when you are doing your journalling reflection afterwards.

Step Three: Exploratory Self-Touch

Once you have had the experience of going through Step Two enough times to feel like you can tolerate and regulate yourself as you connect with your body, it's time to dive a little deeper into direct sexual and sensual stimulation. Again, go through Step One and Step Two, to the point where you feel comfortable and well-regulated emotionally in your body and notice sensations as they arise, and not activated into trauma triggers.

Once you are pretty settled and grounded in your skin, the next step is to add exploratory self-touch and self-caressing with the goal of heightening arousal and moving towards orgasm. Notice what feels arousing and pleasurable and what doesn't. If certain touch (with hands, fingers, objects, or sex toys—whatever feels the most comfortable) feels pleasurable, do it again and then, move along and find other pleasurable sensations. If the touch and caressing, toys, or other ways of stimulating arousal don't feel pleasurable, don't do them; the body and the sexual self is virtually infinite so don't worry if what you think should feel good doesn't, there are lots of ways to find pleasure. Start to notice the rising and falling, rhythms and gentleness, arousal and settling, fear and excitement, all of the spaces and places of reimagining yourself into your body.

At this stage, your goal is to just bookmark what feels pleasurable, neutral, difficult, a no-go zone, triggering, or arousing, as well as any other sensations, feelings, thoughts, or impulses that come along. Move as slowly or quickly over your body as feels right and notice: how do you know that it feels right or not right? When the movement upwards has started to move back to regulated neutral, take some time to reflect on these questions and, do some writing in response.

Step Four: Moving Towards Orgasm

The next step in this coming home to your sexual body exercise is to allow yourself to continue on from Step Three to sensing your way into orgasm, if that feels tolerable and desirable to you. As you move through Step Three and into Step Four, when something feels good, continue to do it until it feels neutral, meh, or even irritating. You might find someone kissing your neck to be really sexy the first three times but after that it might feel irritating and yucky—listen to those feelings and thoughts and follow them.

For people with a clitoris and vagina, you may find that it's hard to figure out how hard to press, how fast to move your fingers, hands, or toys, whether to penetrate yourself vaginally or anally, or how much is too much. That's okay, just go slow, do what feels good, do it again, and follow the impulses and sensations that arise in your body. Keep some lubricant nearby so that you don't lose your arousal if things get a little less slippery than feels good.

For people with a penis that has erections and ejaculations, it's the same. There is a more obvious sign of arousal with an erection than many people with a clitoris and vagina experience so, in many ways, it may feel easier to know what to touch, how hard to touch, and how fast to go. However, when trauma is involved, all bets are off. Just go with what your body is telling you and trust that your body was made for pleasure even if there were experiences that came along to mess that up; we are on the path of reclaiming your right to pleasure in your body.

For people who are going through physical gender transitions that may affect their genitals—hormone blockers, cross sex hormones, phalloplasty, "bottom" surgery—there are even fewer resources out in the world of healing our sexual selves from trauma for trans and non-binary people. However, you were self-aware enough, strong enough, creative enough, and open enough to come alive to your gender identity. If it feels like the right time, you can bring all of those same qualities to your sexual healing. If you are actively transitioning in ways that feel really precious, tender, or tentative, it's also okay to hold yourself carefully and hold back on these exercises until you and your body feel more friendly and loving towards one another.

If you find your way to orgasm, close to orgasm, or even in that zone of feeling sensual and aroused, this is great. If you start to feel triggered into old trauma slow down, breathe, back away, and pull yourself back into the present. Remind yourself that your body belongs to you, your sexuality is your own, and no one gets to intrude on it unless you invite them.

When you've had some time to reflect on this experience, do some journalling with these questions to guide you.

EXERCISE: FINDING YOUR WAY TO YOUR OWN SEXUAL BODY HANDOUT

Step One: Mental Body Scan. What are you sensing, noticing, and thinking, and how does that change from moment to moment?

- Do you feel any sensations?
- Do you know how to notice a sexual or sensual sensation?
- What happens inside you when you do notice a sensual or sexual sensation?
- If you start to feel triggered or activated, are you able to breathe yourself back into a safe zone? Just noticing, tracking, sensing, and being, that is your first step.

When you have taken the time to let yourself be in this exercise, write a bit about what came up for you.

_____

_____

_____

_____

_____

_____

_____

Step Two: Felt Body Scan. Compared to Step One, what do you notice in your Felt Body Scan?

- Do you feel any sensations?
- Do you know how to notice a sexual or sensual sensation?
- What happens inside you when you do notice a sensual or sexual sensation?
- If you started to feel triggered or activated, were you able to breathe yourself back into a safe zone? What did you notice, track, sense, and experience in your body?

_____

_____

_____

_____

_____

_____

_____

Step Three: Exploratory Self-Touch. After you have returned to a regulated neutral state, take some time to reflect on these questions and, do some writing in response.

- What kinds of self-touch felt positive, negative, or neutral?
- How did you know?
- If you felt some arousal, what was it like, did you feel safe, did you feel activated or triggered?
- Were you able to stay with the arousal for long enough to experience any pleasure? What have you noticed about your awareness or lack of awareness of your embodied sexual self?
- Have you felt able to manage any intrusive thoughts, sensations, memories, or other traumatic material? If so, how? If not, how did you get re-regulated?

_____

_____

_____

_____

_____

_____

Journal Reflections: Finding Your Sexuality

JOURNAL REFLECTIONS HANDOUT: FINDING YOUR SEXUALITY

Were you able to stay with your pleasure? How did it feel to stay with it, to move towards heightening it, and to move in the direction of orgasm?

_____

_____

_____

_____

_____

_____

_____

Did you find your way to orgasm? If not, did you stop before you got there? If you made the decision to stop, how did you know when to stop and move back into regulation and self-soothing? If you did find your way to orgasm, what did you notice, feel, sense, think, in the experience of allowing yourself to let down your guard and feel your way into that level of pleasure and arousal?

_____

_____

_____

_____

_____

_____

What were some of the feelings and sensations that arose that were surprising or confusing to you?

_____

_____

_____

_____

_____

_____

_____

What were some of the feelings and sensations that arose that felt old, familiar, and connected to trauma stories for you?

_____

_____

_____

_____

_____

_____

What were some of the feelings and sensations that arose that felt new or different—not connected to trauma?

_____

_____

_____

_____

_____

_____

_____

I'm sure it seems like you've spent a lot of time on your own on this first leg of the sexual healing journey and, well, you have. You can certainly share with your partner your experiences, your journaling reflections, and any thoughts, feelings, sensations, memories, or surprises that came up along the way. And now that it is time to bring your partner into the process, do share as much as you feel safe, comfortable, and ready to share with them. If you are both trauma survivors, and you are both going through these steps, you might want to schedule a weekly check in to share your reflections and experiences if you feel ready and safe to do so.

Navigating Triggers

During the psychoeducational section on sex and sexuality, you had an exercise and handout to begin talking about your sexual triggers, the relationship between triggers and your trauma history, and the impact of sexual triggers on your relationship. Now is the time to deepen those conversations. As we delve into the ways that sex and sexuality can trigger deeply painful traumatic memories, thoughts, feelings, sensations, and ways of feeling about our selves and our bodies, we will work together to develop strategies to manage the triggers and, eventually, to desensitize and diminish them.

Go back to the list of triggers that you developed in the first section on psychoeducation about sex and sexuality. Now that you and your partner have also completed the exercises and sharing in the previous sections on disclosure and trauma processing, you can place your sexual triggers in the context of your traumatic experiences, to help your partner understand the relevant context (Table 3.1). When partners understand the origins of a trigger, there can be a shift from hurt or anger—why doesn't she want me?—to empathy and compassion. Most likely, the trauma memories that unfold through this process will have already been disclosed and discussed through the previous sections, but an extra layer of understanding results when the pieces are brought together to link past trauma to current sexual triggers.

When triggers have been linked to traumatic memories, it is important for you and your partner to talk together about how those triggers have infiltrated your relationship and how this has impacted the two of you and your sexual connection. This is an opportunity for you to really flex your new mentalizing capacities: it can be very painful to hear your partner talking about their trauma and how you, a person who loves them so deeply, could remind them of anything related to such horrors.

Examining each trigger in detail will most likely produce more than one list. There will be one list for triggers that are related to sexual sensations, thoughts, behaviours, and relational stimulations that are unavoidable if you pursue moving through the obstacles to engaging sexually. There may also be a list of those that are avoidable, and possibly a list of triggers connected to sexual activities that are particularly arousing for one or both of you and represent a loss to one of you if the triggers cannot be worked through and desensitized. Many survivors find the very experience of becoming sexually aroused itself to be triggering, so this process needs to start with the basic building blocks of sexual connection. For you and your partner to have a rich and pleasurable sex life, these triggers need to be worked through.

Complete the chart (Table 3.2) for all of your triggers to go into more detail about the specifically sexual elements of your triggers and the impact on your couple relationship and sexual life.

Once you have completed this more in-depth list of sexual triggers, you and your partner can work together to go through the list and develop strategies for each one. For unavoidable triggers, we want to develop a plan to help the two of you safely, slowly, and gradually work your way towards the trigger in a way that feels tolerable, clear, and manageable, until it feels like you don't have to be so careful.

Table 3.1 Exercise: Exploring the Triggers More Deeply

Sexual Trigger	Original Trauma	Response	Impact on Partner and Sexual Encounter	Sharing
Example: my partner becomes aroused more quickly than me, comes towards me with excitement and it sends me back in time.	Example: when my father would come at me to sexually abuse me, he felt out of control and his sexual desire was terrifying and disgusting.	Example: I start to feel terrified, I can't breathe, my brain goes "mushy" and I can't think and then I completely freeze.	Example: my partner looks so hurt and upset but then they get mad and start yelling about how they aren't my perpetrator and it's not fair to make them pay for things they didn't do. Then it all falls apart and we end up sleeping separately.	Example: I have tried to share the trigger and how connected it is to my dad but my partner gets mad. This time I talked about the BASK elements of the trigger and how my body and the memory takes over— it's not that I don't want to be sexual with them! They did seem to get that better.

Table 3.2 Exercise: Developing and Trying Strategies to Reduce Triggers

Sexual Trigger	Impact on Partner and Sexual Encounter	Steps to Reduce Trauma Response	Notes & Progress
Example: my partner becomes aroused more quickly than me, comes towards me with excitement and it sends me back in time.	Example: my partner looks so hurt and upset but then they get mad and start yelling about how they aren't my perpetrator and it's not fair to make them pay for things they didn't do. Then it all falls apart and we end up sleeping apart.	Example: 1) when my partner is moving toward me, they will try to slow down, speak to me and ask if it's okay to come forward. 2) When my partner is close to me and starting to feel aroused, we will hold hands for a moment and do the square breathing exercise to slow down the excitement. 3) If I start to get overwhelmed and shut down, I will raise my hand to ask for a short breathing break.	Example: the first time we tried these steps I got freaked out by my partner speaking to me— like somehow, they were attacking me. But they didn't get upset, we stopped, did square breathing and cuddled and watched a tv show. The second time we tried, my partner was quiet in asking for consent and that worked a lot better. I started to shut down when they started to show me how excited they were, but I was able to put my hand up, we had a breathing break and then I was able to stay present and not end up in a flashback!

An example of an unavoidable trigger would be something like feeling triggered by the sensations of sexual arousal. For avoidable triggers, the two of you can decide if you want to remove these actions, behaviours, sensations, or others from your sexual repertoire or work on the same gradual ramping up as for the unavoidable triggers. An avoidable trigger might be something like vaginal penetration. You can still have very satisfying and pleasurable sexual connection without penetration. However, one or both of you may feel like that is something you would really grieve and so, with lots of talking and navigating, you would work your way towards safely engaging in penetrative sex.

The goal of this process is to create safety in your sexual relationship, to promote sharing and connection so that you can keep communicating when triggers start to flare up, and to find ways for both of you to feel sexually satisfied, safe, and secure. If you feel that your partner fully understands the impact of your trauma, that you've worked together to put strategies in place, and that you can talk about issues as they arise, this goes a long way towards developing a sexual relationship that is flexible, fulfilling, and fun. It also creates the context where mistakes can be made safely and conflict is reduced; if you really feel that your partner understands you and has taken you seriously, when triggers do get aroused it does not feel like an injury but rather an opportunity to use those secure base behaviours and let your partner comfort and soothe you.

Decreasing Sexual Secrets

We worked on sharing secrets earlier in the workbook, and I mentioned at that point that we would get back to sexual secrets in this section. So many survivors carry sexual secrets directly or indirectly related to the specifics of their traumas, including ways to self-regulate or even to avoid sexual intimacy with someone they love and care for. However, if we are going to effectively address issues in your sexual relationship with yourself and your partner, it is important to gradually confront sexual secrets and what I call a bifurcation of sexuality. To bifurcate something is to split it in half. Many, many trauma survivors have secret sexual lives away from their partners, for many reasons, and it is really important to bring these sexual lives together, or at least to navigate consent and shared knowledge between partners of any sexual activities and relationships outside of the couple.

As we have discussed, the sexual challenges of trauma survivors, especially sexual abuse survivors, can run the range from difficulties with initiation and arousal, to deeply entrenched, painfully shameful sexual compulsions and reenactments of past traumas that may be lived out in dangerous and unsafe circumstances. When we become steeped in sexual secrets, we can end up leading a double life involving a distant, disconnected, and traumatically deadened sexual relationship with our partners, along with a shame-filled, chaotic, compulsive, or traumatically reenacted sexual life lived out in dissociative fantasy outside of the relationship.

I have worked with survivors, in individual and couple therapy, where one is living a double life seeking out sexual situations that are directly related to their traumatic sexual experiences. For some people it is about some form of sexual act, sexual stimulation, or sexual feeling that needs to be reenacted over and over again, just to feel like they can live in their skin. For instance, a male-identified sexual abuse survivor who lives a heterosexual life but who hooks up with cisgender men in parks and will only be a passive participant in the sex—this is negotiated before the meeting and clearly stated—without any foreplay or stimulation of his penis, being penetrated without lubricant, without being able to see anything that would give him a relational connection and bring him out of the past: the encounter needs to be painful and shameful. This is not a story I have only heard once or twice I have heard it many, many times. Once the hook up is over, the shame bathes them into disconnection and dissociation, and then they come back to home and partner and family and work, all the things that live in the present. These two lives are separate—the life of a sexual trauma living in the past, and the life of home and family that lives in the present. But healing, especially couple-level sexual healing, can't happen when so much of our sexuality is hiding out in the dark of a park at midnight with strangers who hold our lives in their hands.

For others, the sexual secrets are more independent: compulsive masturbation, compulsive pornography use, masturbation in conjunction with self-injury—as though the very act of sexual pleasure must be punished—and other forms of sexual secrets that are held away from partners. For many, there is also the feeling that their sexual arousal is tied to trauma, that they can't feel aroused or achieve orgasm without going back to the trauma. Bringing oneself back into the memories, feelings, sensations, and experiences of past sexual traumas can be the only way some survivors can achieve orgasm; being in the present with a loving, gentle, attentive partner can feel terrifying, impossible, and anything but sexy. That theme, for many trauma survivors who have experienced sexual trauma in the family, persists—loving someone in a family way is dangerous, sex with someone you love in a family way is bad and shameful, and there is no space for family love, sex, pleasure, and mutual love, respect, generosity, and, most of all, safety and security.

When these kinds of secret sexual lives are happening, partners often have a strong feeling that there are sexual shadows lurking in the corners of their relationship, but the words seem to be hard to find. And, for many reasons, there can be a lot of ambivalence about breaking the silence: maybe knowing more will make things worse, bringing more grief, more anger, or more pain. And, when the secrets come out, partners who have been sheltered from secrets, including secrets about sexual compulsions and reenactments, can feel betrayed. It is important to go slow, to contextualize sexuality that exists outside of a monogamous relationship or sexuality that does not adhere to the agreed upon "rules" of consensual non-monogamy or polyamory.

JOURNAL REFLECTIONS HANDOUT: SEXUAL SECRETS

Are you carrying sexual secrets from your partner? If so, do you feel safe putting them down on paper or, at least, giving them a code name?

_____

_____

_____

_____

_____

_____

_____

How are your sexual secrets connected to your trauma? Are they direct—like the actual sexual activities are a reflection of your trauma? Are they indirect—i.e., there is something about how these sexual secrets make you feel that is connected to your trauma?

_____

_____

_____

_____

_____

_____

_____

How does it feel to keep and hold these sexual secrets from your partner?

_____

_____

_____

_____

_____

_____

_____

Do you have any sense that your partner might be holding sexual secrets from you? If so, what causes you to believe this?

_____

_____

_____

_____

_____

_____

Have you ever tried to share any of these with your partner? If so, how far did you get and how did that go? If not, what has held you back from breaking the silence?

_____

_____

_____

_____

_____

_____

What do you imagine is the impact of these sexual secrets on your relationship? How does it feel to reflect on this?

_____

_____

_____

_____

_____

_____

Do you feel that your sexual relationship with your partner is distinct and separate from your secret sexual life? What does that feel like? What are the sensations, feelings, thoughts, and embodied impulses that go along with feeling like you have these two distinct sexual lives?

_____

_____

_____

_____

_____

_____

What "mechanisms" do you use to keep these sexual secrets away from your self while you are living your life with your partner? Do you have a knowing of these secrets while you are with your partner or are they kept in a separate part of your self and your mind? Do you feel that you are living in a state of dissociation to keep these secrets?

_____

_____

_____

_____

_____

_____

What do you imagine your partner would think, feel, experience, or want to do, if you were to share more about your sexual secrets? How do you imagine this to be true?

_____

_____

_____

_____

_____

_____

_____

How do you imagine you would feel after sharing your sexual secrets with your partner?

_____

_____

_____

_____

_____

_____

Are there any no-go zones for you when you think about sharing these parts of your sexual self with your partner? If so, what aspects of your sexual secrets do you feel are not on the table for sharing?

_____

_____

_____

_____

_____

_____

This is another area where having a DCTCT couple therapist to work with as you navigate these challenging processes would be quite helpful. If you cannot find someone who has expertise in working with couples dealing with trauma, if you can't afford to work with someone in this way, or if you simply don't want to bring a therapist into your relationship, it will be really important to go slowly, carefully, and err on the side of caution. The goal is to bring you closer, not to explode your relationship.

First, once you have completed the above reflections independently, take some time to reflect on where you might start. Perhaps you feel that your partner will be able to tolerate hearing about a separate life of masturbation or pornography use, but you are still feeling a lot of fearfulness, shame, or even experiencing these relationships with your sexuality as very separate through dissociation or traumatic reliving. If so, can you set aside a time to share this with your partner in a way that fully embraces the complexity and context that will help your partner hear what you are sharing? For instance, helping a partner understand how these sexual secrets are tied to your trauma can be a part of decreasing the sense of secrecy, any feelings of hurt and betrayal, or as though you are "cheating" on them in this double life. You probably aren't ready to share any sexual secrets if you aren't ready to work towards letting them go or negotiating a way to integrate them into your relationship clearly, consciously, and intentionally, so spend a lot of time reflecting on that question before moving towards sharing any sexual secrets.

As with all of the other sharing experiences in the workbook, set aside a time, and make sure that you have a plan to share what you need to share in a contextualized way. It's okay to write it down and read it to your partner if that feels less likely to become confusing or overwhelming. If you can make an expression, clearly, and intentionally, about your desire to become closer through this sharing, that would be great. This sharing is for you, to let go of the shame and pain of the separateness and dividedness in your sexual life. But this sharing is also for your partner, to bring them in closer, to demonstrate your desire and willingness to work on your sexual life together, and to help them understand and contextualize any feelings and thoughts that they might have had about challenges in your sexual relationship.

Share the story of your sexual secret with your partner slowly, clearly, empathically, and responsibly. As painful as it is, we aren't responsible for what was done to us, but we are responsible for our own healing and for not hurting the people we love. When you've shared your secret, give your partner as much time as they need to take it in, feel the feelings, think the thoughts, and connect the dots with any suspicions they may already have had about your sexual secret. Give them space to breathe and, when it seems that they are with you, ask them how they feel; what they are thinking; and what you can do to help them to feel, in a deeply embodied way, how much you're sharing this with them is about your desire to be closer, safer, and more secure in your attachment and sexual connection.

When it is time for disclosures of these sexual secrets, it is important that they be well-timed and carefully prepared, with a focus on your shiny new emotion regulation and mentalizing skills, while preserving the newness of your growing earned security in your attachment with one another. You will need to decide how much to disclose. On the one hand, secrets stand between you and your partner and will get in the way of rebuilding strong and secure attachment. On the other hand, some secrets have the potential to devastate your partner. It is important to reflect on the question of whether your partner needs to know all of the nitty-gritty details. If there are potential health related concerns—such as engaging in unprotected sex with an affair partner or hook up—this *needs* to be disclosed to protect the wellbeing of your partner and so both of you can get tested for STIs. It is often enough to share the model scene of the sexual secret: enough that the secret is unveiled but not so much that the partner is torn open. Once sexual secrets have been shared, it is essential to make enough time to explore the injuries to both partners in the relationship and to the relationship itself, time to explore the possibility of healing. Sexual secrets have a unique potential to cause pain; how can a partner tolerate not feeling desired while their partner is engaging in a secret sexual life elsewhere, even if that life is unwanted and disavowed.

If there is more than one sexual secret and these are held by both partners: again, take the time and space you need to share slowly, carefully, and lovingly. Take turns sharing and give a lot of time between disclosure to give you enough time and space to let things digest. If your partner needs some time on their own to process, reflect, and return to you for debriefing, give them the time—it's your turn to hold onto your fear and anxiety about your connection.

JOURNAL REFLECTIONS HANDOUT: SHARING SEXUAL SECRETS

How did it feel to share your sexual secret(s)?

_____

_____

_____

_____

_____

_____

What do you notice about your sense of self, connection with past-present-and-future in your relationship, and your feelings, sensations, impulses and thoughts about your relationship, as you move out of having shared this secret?

_____

_____

_____

_____

_____

_____

_____

How did your partner respond to the sharing of your sexual secret? Was this what you imagined? If so, how did you find your way to that imagining? If not, what was different and how do you understand it?

_____

_____

_____

_____

_____

_____

_____

If your partner shared a sexual secret with you, what was that like for you? Were you surprised? If so, how do you now understand why that secret was kept away from your relationship? If not, why do you feel that you had a sense of something happening?

_____

_____

_____

_____

_____

_____

_____

How does knowing the sexual secret change how you feel, sense, and think about your relationship, your closeness, your sexual connection, and any other things that arise for you in digesting this new information?

_____

_____

_____

_____

_____

_____

_____

Reducing Bifurcation

Once the secrets have been told, and your partner is brought into your hidden sexual life, healing the divide between the two sides of your sexuality can begin. Early sexual conditioning through sexual abuse is powerful and not easily changed. In fact, it is unlikely that sexual conditioning to traumatic stimuli will change. For instance, a young child is often groomed by a perpetrator by being shown love, affection, and attention, given gifts, affirmed, and held tenderly, at least at first. Oftentimes the perpetrator will groom that child by making the sexual abuse pleasurable—by touching or kissing gently, by slowly arousing the child. It's hard to understand, but this form of grooming can be particularly confusing to a young child—why does this feel good when I know it is so bad? And, on the opposite side of things, as often with cisgender pubertal boys being abused, a perpetrator might be rough, cause pain and damage to the young boy's body, but bodies are bodies, and that young boy may still experience an erection, orgasm, and ejaculation, through the stimulation of their penis and genitals. For this boy, pleasure becomes tied with the pain and shame of abuse, and that can be really hard to uncouple.

Turning towards our partners to have our sexual needs met, rather than away and into a dissociated double sexual life, involves finding ways to develop a sexual life together that both of you find arousing and satisfying. It can feel confusing if a partner has linked pain with arousal or penetration by a same sex partner to their capacity to orgasm and ejaculate, while being in a committed heterosexual relationship with a cisgender woman. However, when secrets are broken down and the partner is brought into discussions about sexual needs and struggles, it becomes possible for the couple to navigate and negotiate how they will deal with conditioned sexual arousal that does not fit into their sexual comfort zone.

Once you have shared your secrets and spent time working on any anger, hurt, and betrayal for the long-term impacts of being in a relationship with someone who had been hiding sexual secrets, there is space for rebuilding.

If one of your sexual secrets involved feeling aroused, masturbating, and coming to orgasm through watching a particular kind of pornography, would it feel possible to include your partner in that activity? How would your partner feel about this form of pornography? If that would feel uncomfortable, shameful, or even distasteful, is there a kind of pornography that both of you could enjoy that would be a kind of middle zone compromise?

If your sexual secret involved some form of reenacted sexual trauma, see if you and your partner can talk through the traumas that are being reenacted, work on the triggers and how certain kinds of traumas have become linked in your sexual arousal, take those apart, and find a way to express the desire that is palatable to both partners and no longer leaves the partner with the linked arousal in the dust of a sexuality tied to the past. For instance, some couples find ways to engage in role playing activities, using consensual forms of pain or control, or even leaving space for a partner to dip in and out of a conditioned memory or fantasy to help them feel aroused at the same time as staying connected to one another.

For some couples, moving towards clear, conscious, consensual, non-monogamy to allow for space to explore sexual fantasies, desires, or needs that cannot be met within the couple relationship may be an option for addressing conditioned sexual responses that don't "fit" in the relationship or for the partner. Consensual, ethical non-monogamy or polyamory requires that you have very clear communication about what is and isn't okay, how to protect against STIs, and how much and how often to share about your other relationships and sexual partners.

The solutions to sexual challenges will be different for every couple. They can begin by working on becoming comfortable and knowledgeable about your own sexual self and responses; share and work through triggers to bring more regulation, comfort, clarity, context, and safety to move into vulnerability and arousal with your partner; and work through sexual secrets that might be leading to double sexual lives that rob you of closeness, security, and safety in your sexual relationship. All of these are steps to bringing change and growth to your sexual relationship. Whether you move closer into monogamy and bring your sexual secrets into your relationship with your partner, or if you move closer in emotional and attachment connection while building a strong foundation for exploring these aspects of your sexual life with other partners through clearly communicated and contracted non-monogamy, the goal is reducing painful separateness and avoidance of sexual pleasure in your partnership.

Breaking the Seal

Many couples who come to see me are struggling with a vacuum where their sexual relationship once lived. It is not unusual for me to hear that a couple has gone years without any kind of sexual contact. For most, this isn't something they are happy about, but it is something they have kind of accepted, and yet feel hopeless about. This vacuum arises out of all of the issues we've discussed above, including not being able to find their way through all of the triggers and tumult of trauma that makes body to body to contact with another human being feel terrifying, traumatizing, and altogether impossible. Without the words or the self and co-regulatory capacities, and often filled with overwhelming shame, these couples seem to shove the topic of sex into the shadows and move along with survival. It is often a surprise to these couples when I ask about their sexual relationship, as though I will implicitly understand that the silence renders their sexualities invisible. However, with a little loosening of the stays of hopelessness and dissociated despair, it becomes clear that many of these couples also feel a deep sadness and yearning for a safe rekindling of their sexual connection.

For other trauma survivors, the issue is not just the trauma triggers or the feelings of embodied vulnerability and terror of the emotional danger that accompanies the risk of opening up to a sexuality that includes another human being but also how sex and love and family became congealed in their childhoods. There is a delicate dance that unfolds as children grow through puberty and into adulthood. Not only do our bodies change in dramatic ways but our awareness of our sexual selves develops along with our curiosity about those to whom we are attracted and all of the experimentation, confusion, creativity, and sometimes chaos, that goes along with becoming sexual beings. This is a gradual unfolding that happens in plain sight and, when our families are healthy and well, can be mirrored, acknowledged, supported, and held by our caregivers with a healthy dose of good boundaries and privacy.

For trans and non-binary youth, moving into puberty—especially if it isn't safe to be out to family and to access gender affirming care—can be ever more complicated and painful; it can engender the desire to run and hide our sexual bodies as they grow and develop. When our families do not have healthy boundaries, when there are sexual intrusions and violations, and when we live in homes where we are ridiculed, tormented, teased, or otherwise taunted about our development, our sexuality can get mushed up and confounded with all of the family mess that is happening around us.

Imagine how challenging it is to be a pubescent girl, cisgender, emerging into a new and sexually developing body, in a home where she is also being stalked and predated upon by someone who should be caring for her and protecting her. When a caregiver intrudes sexually by making comments about an adolescent's developing body, through sexual abuse, through exposing a youth to porn or other explicit sexual material, they mix up the family, the caregiver, the safety, and the sex and sexuality, into a very confusing blend of mushy yuck that seems better to avoid than dive into. So, when we find ourselves in adult romantic relationships that, over time, morph into family relationships, there can be a really confusing struggle for survivors of what is called intrafamilial (intra—in—familial—in the family) sexual abuse and other forms of violence. How can we find a way to allow our normal, beautiful sexualities breathe and expand and explore, when family equals danger and the boundaries of caregivers—who are supposed to be non-sexual and simply caring for us, as children—are all confused and violated?

And, well, it can just feel really weird trying to approach our partners sexually after going about life and living, sometimes for years: doing the laundry, making the meals, brushing the teeth, sharing a bathroom, and all of the stuff of life that can feel so very much not sexy. Between all of the traumatic ways that our bodies close up, hide away, and protect; all of the ways our traumas become embodied in memories and sensations that can be triggered by the vulnerability of closeness and sexual connection; and the struggle of finding a safe way to be family and lovers at the same time, there are a lot of obstacles for trauma survivors in developing and maintaining a vibrant sexual life. So, things can fall into slumber and then it's just weird and hard and awkward to wake it all up again.

After working through the various challenges and exercises discussed above, that's sometimes where we are left—we've talked about the triggers but how do we get started again? How do we break the seal that has been hiding our sexual connection and bring it back to life?

For many couples, the act of working through those exercises and having these challenging discussions is enough to reignite their sexual connection. For others, there needs to be more lubrication for the wheels to get going. And for many others, there are relationship wounds around the topic of how to get the wheels going—one partner always initiating, one partner feeling that the other wasn't present or was very much in a traumatized space during sex, a partner feeling that they are just going along because they "have to", a partner hiding all of the ways that they are triggered and finding themselves in a non-mentalizing space of blaming their partner for their trauma instead of having the challenging conversations with them.

These wounds also have to be talked through and worked through. These are wounds that can be worked through using the Learned Emotional Experiences exercise or the

Mentalizing Questions reflections to help you get started in discussing your relationship injuries in ways that are a bit contained and structured. This is an opportunity to try your co-regulation skills and your mentalizing capacities as you try to hold yourself gently, share openly, and maintain your empathy for your partner without falling into shame yourself.

As you come to work through the ways in which your sexual relationship slipped away, it is an opportunity to talk about how to reconstruct your sexual relationship with openness, clarity, honesty, and equality. This is also a time to let go of old fantasies about what a sexual relationship is all about—there are no mind readers on the Relation-Ship! Your partner can only learn about what you want and like by you communicating it to them; there is no magic here. Communication can come in many forms, but it still needs to be clear, direct, and specific, similar to our Secure Base Behaviours. This is a time to talk about your fantasies, your desires, your hopes, and your fears. It is a time to be brave and explore the ways in which you are very compatible and not compatible. It can be a time to talk about the things you'd like to try and to negotiate compromises that you can all feel good about.

Once you have found your way through these challenging conversations: again, for many couples, that is enough heat to get the fires burning again and sexual connection grows out of the direct, specific, and clear nature of your discussions about your sexual desires, fantasies, and hopes and fears.

What do you do, though, when all of these conversations don't get you feeling warm all over and ready to go? Well, sometimes it's just necessary to make a date, agree to show up at the appointed time, and start slowly and work your way up. While it may seem contrived and not very romantic to plan a date for reengaging sexually, it is clear, direct, and specific. Sunday after lunch, Tuesday after dinner, Friday at lunch when the kids are at school and you have a work from home shared day—it doesn't matter when, so long as you both feel like you can relax, be present, and not feel rushed. If that option feels too contrived, you could go with a random number generator on the computer to tell you what date and time to go for it, or even a pick a card game where the person who picks the highest card has to initiate some sexual contact within the next 48 hours.

Whatever you do to break the seal, it is important to go slow, to talk and to listen, and to have signals for start and stop so that you can both be present in your bodies and in the connection between you, throughout. You can have words that mean stop and go—even "stop" and "go"—a hand signal, or a song. The important part is that if you are starting to feel like you need to slow down, stop, talk, or just hold your partner for a while to get grounded, that whatever you have chosen as a signal is something you know you can do if you are feeling spacy, triggered, frightened, or generally overwhelmed. By this point in the workbook, you will have a good sense of what you are able to hold onto at those moments, so hold yourself and your partner in gentleness and compassion and don't make anything mean more than it is. If you need to stop, stop, but, don't just walk away: stay with one another and start again when you are both feeling like you are grounded, regulated, and present in your bodies and connection.

So, armed with a date and a time, safe words, and important conversations under your belts, simply start slow. Take turns taking five minutes each to ask your partner to touch you in a way that feels just right. Whether that is a gentle stroking of the inside of your arm or a neck massage, choose something that you have a good sense will feel sensual and pleasant, and then switch. The next time you have a date make it ten minutes and expand the touch into more of your bodies. It's okay if you still feel like you need to touch over clothes and you aren't ready to get naked; take your time. Again, it can take as long as it takes: even a turtle gets to the finish line. As you continue to work towards breaking the seal, you are learning more about one another, what feels good, what you like and how you like it. Go slow but steady until you do feel ready to have skin on skin contact and move on into more and more, arousal, connection, sensuality, and more direct and explicit sexual touch and contact. If it takes a year before you are lying breathless and naked in one another's arms, that's okay. The goal is to get there in your own time without losing any of your sense of safety, security, openness, and comfort along the way.

Dyadic Traumatic Reenactment

The last section in Stage Three is about working on Dyadic Traumatic Reenactments (DTR). In the psychoeducation section, we looked at your negative cycles and how trauma can get stuck in them. In this section we are going to take that a bit further; we will work on some skills and ways to reflect and regulate that will help you start to disentangle the past from the present. We have taken some steps towards this already, when we disclosed and processed some traumatic experiences and memories and worked on triggers in our connection and sexual relationship.

The challenge of the DTR is similar to the struggles we can have with being aware of our IWMs for attachment. Remember that our evolution has primed us for survival, and that has meant building brains that are really good at noticing bad and dangerous stuff and not quite so good at noticing things that are great: i.e., not bad and dangerous. That is what we are up against when we try to shift our ways of being attached to earned security with our partner. Where DTRs are concerned, we are also up against something similar in that when we are in those negative cycles and we are dealing with trauma getting all tied up in there, our brains don't separate the past from the present—the dangerous very very bad thing that is happening *right now* may actually be a very very bad and dangerous thing that happened a long time ago, and *is not* happening right now. It's really hard for us to know this difference, in the moment that we are being pulled into all of the feelings and fears that come from the past.

DTRs are another place, like attachment, where we can *know* that something is a certain way—like that we are being hijacked by our trauma when we get pulled into a negative cycle with our partner—but we also can't get out of it, change it, or know what we know when we are in the tangled mess of it.

Journal Reflections: DTRs

Return to your responses to the journalling prompts from the section on DTRs in the first section of the workbook and review these before responding to these journal prompts.

DOI: 10.4324/9781003330950-24

JOURNAL REFLECTIONS HANDOUT: DYADIC TRAUMATIC REENACTMENT

How have your awareness of, thoughts, feelings, and beliefs about your negative cycle shifted over the course of completing the other sections in the workbook?

_____

_____

_____

_____

_____

_____

_____

What have you noticed that has shifted in how you and your partner get pulled into your negative cycle over the course of completing the other sections in the workbook?

_____

_____

_____

_____

_____

_____

_____

Have you noticed any changes in the frequency, duration, and intensity of moments of being pulled into and stuck in your negative cycle? If so, what, in particular, have you noticed?

_____

_____

_____

_____

_____

_____

_____

How has it changed, to be "in" your negative cycle, over the course of completing the workbook? What do you notice is different about how you feel, your ability to self and co-regulate with your partner while in the cycle, your capacity to maintain your mentalizing and continue to reflect on yourself and empathize with your partner? What other changes feel important to you?

_____

_____

_____

_____

_____

_____

When you do find yourself in your negative cycle with your partner, what do you notice about being able to stop it, pull back, and focus on what is important to explore? How successful are the strategies that you have been using to work on your cycle, together?

_____

_____

_____

_____

_____

_____

When moving into reflecting on the DTR, what have you noticed about what aspects of your trauma get triggered into your negative cycle and how it feels when this happens?

_____

_____

_____

_____

_____

_____

When looking at the concrete DTR—the things that are being clearly repeated—versus the more symbolic DTR—the things that are more like a sensory or embodied repetition, what have you noticed that has changed since you started working through the workbook?

_____

_____

_____

_____

_____

_____

_____

What do you notice about your awareness of past and present being fused together when you are in your DTR? Has that awareness changed since you started working on the exercises in the workbook?

_____

_____

_____

_____

_____

_____

_____

How have the strategies that you have been using impacted the frequency, intensity, and duration, of getting pulled into DTRs and being able to get yourselves out of them?

_____

_____

_____

_____

_____

_____

_____

Working Through the DTRs Together

You have done the first step in this work: the understanding and knowledge. You've reflected on how and why your negative cycle pulls you and your partner in, and you've reflected on how trauma plays a role in this. You've reflected and explored how your past trauma gets stuck in your negative cycle through both awareness of the concrete elements—for instance, at a really concrete level maybe your mother used to scream at you and your siblings and now when your partner yells you become completely overwhelmed and feel like the little girl you were when you had no power or control. And at that more symbolic level, perhaps when you were experiencing sexual abuse, your aunt might get really big and threaten to tell your mother what a "bad girl" you were if you ever threatened to tell anyone what was happening. For your survival you may have needed to shrink down into a fiery ball of smallness and focus on getting right in the middle of that ball and disappearing. And so, when your partner is angry with you, they can start to tell you things about yourself that trigger all of those feelings of shame and anger and you might just find yourself back in that little fiery ball, wanting to escape and, feeling all of those intolerable feelings as your partner continues to move towards you.

These insights can be painful, especially when we feel so helpless to build space between the present and the past and change the power of the repetition that gets stuck in our negative cycle. These insights, while painful and sometimes shameful, can be achieved because they relate something knowable to something else that is thinkable. I know about the context and content of my trauma, and I know about the context and content of my couple relationship and our cycle, and I can think my way into connecting those two things.

However, by trying to articulate this clearly, I do not in any way mean to suggest that it is easy or simple. It can be immensely painful to realize that the partner you thought was so different from your abuser, on many levels, is so much like your abuser. For many of us, especially those of us who have had a lot of therapy, these two steps will come somewhat naturally—we will already have the skills to tackle the tasks of figuring these out. Where the rubber hits the road, however, is at the third level, that which is outside of our awareness and is reenacted moment by moment in ways that cannot be known in words or felt in ways that distinguish the present as separate from the past. This third level is like a live stream of trauma superimposed onto the present in your relationship, and this is where things get tough. Survivors and partners often feel frustrated and helpless as they try to implement change based on knowledge and insight, without success. The thoughts and feelings, sensations and shadows do not allow the past to be pried out from the present; the couple has trouble even identifying how they are reliving the past in waking life because it feels indistinguishable from now...it feels like an immense, painful, horrible now, still felt as present in the present.

What does all of this mean? How can we liberate ourselves from the vice-like grip of the past? As discussed in the section on shifting attachment, aspects of this powerful pull are conscious and knowable, while others remain outside of our awareness and are, therefore, not knowable in a conscious, thinking way. The biggest challenge is that, to change them, DTRs must be brought alive, in the present, so that they can be stripped down and examined in their emotional reality. If you are working with a DCTCT therapist, they will help you to smell, taste, feel, and see the past and to disentangle that which has been held outside of awareness as it is brought into painful relief. Focusing on words and what is observable in your current negative cycle may actually make the unconscious DTR even more stuck and rigid. While working at the first and second levels of the cycle is important, eventually the cycle must be experienced in the immediate moment, to expose what is being repeated here and now and to make space to explore the way this DTR is alive for you and your partner in real time.

As dissociated emotions, sensations, thoughts, and relational expectancies come up in your cycle, you and your partner can start by working on regulating your emotional arousal, tolerating new information about yourselves and your traumas built on the insights you have developed, and acknowledging and processing the impact of any new memories that emerge in your DTR as you continue to work them through. These experiences of emergence can help you wrestle free of the hold of the past on the present negative cycle, as its power slowly fades away. Over time, with enough runs through the process, the unsymbolized can be symbolized and the past's pull on the negative interaction cycle begin to loosen. Change happens slowly as consciousness dawns over strong feelings and deep-seated trauma memories; this allows both of you the space to reflect, regulate, mentalize, and respond to one another in the present without being drawn into cycles of the past. Through these new experiences, new relational expectancies will gradually emerge, allowing for a more fluid expression of new security-promoting attachment behaviours that had been held back by the "stuckness" of the DTR.

Drawing on an example from the DCTCT treatment manual, Chris and Camille, a young couple dealing with the impacts of both of their traumas on their relationship, were able to fairly easily establish the first level of understanding of their negative cycle, a cognitive understanding. Chris was relentlessly and anxiously pursuing Camille from his Fearful Avoidant attachment lens while Camille would withdraw at the first sign of pressure, reflecting her Avoidant attachment lens and, all the while, reinforcing Chris's anxiety and pursuit. As one pursues, the other withdraws, and around and around we go, the more withdrawal, the more pursuit and vice versa.

Over time, through the DCTCT process, Chris and Camille were able to develop the second level of understanding, the deeper level of insight. Chris understood that he became fearful of rejection because of the difficult cycles of rejection and abandonment he experienced in his family of origin, which were tightly embodied as an automatic assumption in times of need. Camille continued to experience feelings of fear, waiting for danger and betrayal, and emotional dysregulation, as a present-day echo of her trauma of parents who could not, and possibly would not, respond to her overwhelming distress. Chris's intrusive pursuit triggered her into states of dysregulation and withdrawal. Chris and Camille could identify this cycle and could understand it in relation to the longer term-impacts of trauma. At the beginning, neither Camille nor Chris could tolerate the idea that the past was still living in the present, or that their cycle was deeply influenced by the emotional responses, sensations, thoughts, and actions associated with living as though the trauma was still happening. Chris was still struggling with reenacting this historical cycle as "real", expecting abandonment at every turn and needing to be vigilant now, not then. Camille was reenacting the horribly painful experience of never having her needs for care met by those who should have protected and supported her. Her parents' inability to tolerate her distress and support her following a sexual assault was living in her expectation of being failed, but she had no conscious awareness of the origins of these expectations: they were simply there in real time. This aspect of the negative pattern was not conscious for either partner.

Exercise: Noticing and Naming

Using the reflections and responses to journal prompts from the first section and just above, start out by outlining the linearity of your DTR. This is an exercise that both of you can do together. What is the beginning, middle, and end...and at what point does the DTR get activated? Are you both able to have some conscious awareness of that or are you still a bit stuck in the past when it is happening?

EXERCISE: NOTICING AND NAMING HANDOUT

In as much detail as you are able, identify the triggers to your negative cycle, your attachment needs that get activated, your feelings towards one another and yourselves, and the general feeling of the cycle.

_____

_____

_____

_____

_____

_____

Moving into the second level of awareness, try to notice, know, tolerate, reflect upon, and pull yourself out of the impact of the trauma on your negative cycle. In as much detail as you are able, what things get your negative cycle going? What happens as it starts to escalate? When does the DTR creep in and how does it "end"?

_____

_____

_____

_____

_____

_____

Just working at the level of your thinking, how does your negative cycle replicate aspects of your trauma, concretely? (E.g. a yelling parent and a yelling partner, an abuser that left you crying on the floor in the middle of nowhere and a partner who walks away from you when you are crying and in significant distress.)

_____

_____

_____

_____

_____

_____

What is the first moment that either of you are aware that something related to past trauma is ramping up and starting to hijack your interaction?

_____

_____

_____

_____

_____

_____

What do you notice in your body, sensations, images, feelings, and any other ways of knowing, that helps you notice that something from the past is present in your negative cycle at that moment?

_____

_____

_____

_____

_____

_____

What do you notice in your partner's body, verbal and non-verbal communications, and any other ways of knowing, that helps you notice that they may be slipping into something from the past in your negative cycle at that moment?

_____

_____

_____

_____

_____

_____

Are either or both of you able to hold that awareness, share it with one another, and pause for reflection? If so, how is that? If not, what do you think is making that a challenge?

_____

_____

_____

_____

_____

_____

Exercise: Accepting and Acknowledging

There is a risk, here, that one or both of you will start to feel that your partner is undermining or diminishing your distress by drawing it back to the DTR. This is really important. The goal of identifying, embodying, and shifting the DTR is to give you the space you need to be able to address, acknowledge, and resolve legitimate conflicts and distress. If, by exploring the DTR, you start to feel like your legitimate concern or distress is being denied, go back to Step One and work on identifying the cycle, identifying the DTR, and then try again. If the DTR is navigated well, it should give you more space, more acknowledgement, and more validation for what is happening in the present—not less.

EXERCISE: ACCEPTING AND ACKNOWLEDGING HANDOUT

How could your partner signal to you that some of the feelings, sensations, images, and other aspects of the DTR, are feeling activated and alive in an interaction—while it is happening? Can you think of language, actions, or ways of gazing at one another, that might help you to hear and tolerate, slow down and reflect on the signal?

_____

_____

_____

_____

_____

_____

_____

What might you notice, in the cycle, in your partner, that might trigger an awareness in you that the DTR is off and running?

_____

_____

_____

_____

_____

_____

_____

Based on how you know one another, what do you imagine might be a helpful and effective way of signalling to them your awareness that the DTR has hijacked your negative cycle?

_____

_____

_____

_____

_____

_____

_____

In a similar vein to the work we did on attachment, we need to find ways to attend to the evidence that disconfirms the sensations, feelings, images, thoughts, beliefs, and other aspects of the experience that keep the hold of past trauma spinning in the present negative cycle. One of the ways to do that, very similarly to how we start to shift our attachment expectations, is to find ways—which you negotiate *before* you are in the cycle and DTR—to hold one another in suspension over and outside of the pull of the past.

For Chris and Camille, it felt almost insulting to them that I would express curiosity about how trauma and the past might be nudging its way into their negative cycle. It was clear that for both of them, their cycle was informed by Chris's historical experiences with parents that were alternating between yelling and screaming and shutting him out in silence, for weeks at a time, and Camille's expectation that caregivers and people she needs to support her will absolutely be incompetent and unhelpful. Both partners were stuck in their stuckness—it all felt very real—Camille *was* shutting Chris out and abandoning him in his times of distress and Chris *was* an incompetent non-empathic or caring partner.

In some ways, when we are climbing this last big mountain, it is another way to face the realities of how our traumas have impacted us. If what happened then wasn't so bad but what is happening now is *really bad*, then, perhaps, we can have a little control and power over all of the feelings, sensations, images, and impulses, and thoughts that are happening because they are based on what *is happening now*. If we accept that much of what we are experiencing in the distressing interaction with our partner is being primed by history and trauma, that can feel really yucky and infuriating and hopeless. However, we simply need to reframe it: we can do something about it, and the something we need to do about it is putting the past where it belongs—back in the past—as part of the ongoing work of trauma recovery. As long as all those aspects of that experience are clinging tightly to your couple relationship, it is impossible to bring them into the light, work through them, and, eventually, to let them go so that you can have a relationship that is just about you and your partner and the hard work you have done to build this closeness and learn how to resolve real issues that are really arising in the now.

Eventually, Chris and Camille were able to get to a place of acknowledging and accepting the DTR of how past traumatic experiences and relationships were alive but...it stayed stuck. That stuckness reflects how hard it is to whisper just a little bit of space between the past and the present—the crazy glue of the DTR makes it feel nothing but reality in *this* moment. If you are working with a DCTCT therapist, they will guide you through this process and these exercises can enhance your work. If you are working on your own, it can be more challenging to build the kind of embodied awareness that goes deeper than cognitive insight. Follow the exercises, co-regulate, and draw upon your understanding of the stories you have shared, the triggers you have navigated, and the attachment earned security that you are building.

Exercise: Catching and Changing

Now that you have moved through these steps and are able to notice and name, acknowledge and accept how the past is alive in your negative cycle through the DTR, it's time to start catching it and changing it. This involves a leap of faith, trusting, at least intellectually, that you and your partner are both working towards the same goal of being able to resolve and reconnect when real conflicts arise that need to be addressed. Holding onto that—at least at the level of your thinking—can help you hold yourself both *in*—in the experience with your partner and your self that is sucking you into the past, and *out*—outside of the gravitational pull of your DTR.

EXERCISE: CATCHING AND CHANGING HANDOUT

Having completed the journal reflections above, can you and your partner make a list of the specific characteristics of the DTR as it gets activated in your couple? Is there one of you who pursues? If so—who, how, why, when, and what does that feel like in your body, what are the thoughts, sensations, images, and impulses that that partner experiences?

_____

_____

_____

_____

_____

_____

Is there one of you that avoids, runs away, withdraws, when pulled into your negative cycle and DTR? If so—who, how, why, when, and what does that feel like in your body? What are the thoughts, sensations, images, and impulses that that partner experiences?

_____

_____

_____

_____

_____

Have you identified how your pursuit and withdrawal are linked in the *now* in relation to both of your attachment styles—expectations and IWMs? If so—describe this in detail for both of you.

_____

_____

_____

_____

_____

_____

Reflecting back on your earlier responses to the journal reflection prompts, what aspects of your past relationships, attachment experiences, traumas, and embodied expectations in connection, can you pull out as being superimposed over the negative cycle?

_____

_____

_____

_____

_____

Can you identify how these might increase the intensity, level of conflict and distress, and decrease reflection and mentalizing when you are drawn into a DTR? If so, please write this out in as much detail as you are able.

_____

_____

_____

_____

_____

_____

Now, here's the hard part—let's put all of these pieces together and into action.

Table 3.3 DTR Worksheet

Triggering Conflict	Negative Cycle	DTR	Strategies Attempted	Outcome	Strategies to try next time
Example: partner A left out the dinner from the evening before and now it is ruined, and couple was planning on eating this for two days.	Example: partner B is angry and starts to pursue partner A to express their distress about finances, waste, and... how they ALWAYS do these things!!	Example: partner B comes from a traumatizing family of substance abusers living with constant food and housing insecurity. Partner A comes from a family that blamed them for everything. They were diagnosed with ADHD, which gave the family the "right" to make them the scapegoat.	Example: 1) whichever partner is able to calls a time out and says "we're in it again". 2) Both partners do a square breathing exercise together. 3) Both partners take a moment to reflect on their own trauma and how it might be creeping in. 4) Couple talks about this directly. 5) Couple addresses the actual question of what to have for dinner.	Example: step 1 went well, partner B was able to call a time out. Step 2 was okay, we were able to do a breathing exercise but we couldn't do it together. Step 3 was sort of okay: we were able to slow down for a moment but then partner A cut it short and hopped back onto the DTR. Step 4 didn't work well; it just fell apart and we were back at it but...we didn't go as deeply back into the hole.	Example: Next time, have a timer for step 3—longer time and externally imposed. For step 4, maybe next time we could journal, separately, about what is going on and then come back together to see if we can talk about it directly without falling back in?

Triggering Conflict	Negative Cycle	DTR	Strategies Attempted	Outcome	Strategies to try next time

Exercise: DTR Worksheet

It will take a long time for these conversations to iron themselves out, to be smooth and comfortable, and for your awareness of how the past is overlaying so much of your conflicts in the negative cycle and DTR. That's okay. Keep working through the worksheet in Table 3.3. If some new strategy works, excellent. If not, don't despair, keep going and try something else. Each time you try, you will be strengthening the muscle that is your relational capacity to hold yourself (your thoughts, feelings, sensations, impulses, and memories) and to hold your partner (and their thoughts, feelings, sensations, impulses, and memories) in mind. Each time you try, you will improve your capacity to work together with your partner at becoming more able to navigate these painful cycles. And, each time, you will move closer to being able to build the space you need between the past and the present to allow you to work through the very real problem that you are dealing with in the present and the very painful story of the past. Both of these are important and deserve their own time and space.

None of this healing from trauma stuff is easy but, as much as it's awful, no one else is going to do it for us. When we do make small changes, a little at a time, time after time, we are reclaiming ourselves, our lives, and our loves, from what was done to us, and we are one step closer to the past becoming a series of sad and painful memories that no longer have control over our daily lives and our relationship with our partner.

Consolidation

All handouts are available for download at www.routledge.com/9781032362465.

DOI: 10.4324/9781003330950-25

Consolidation

The goal of Stage Four is to consolidate everything that has come before. The process of DCTCT is challenging and at times gruelling, but we trauma survivors are remarkably resilient: we have to be. If you have made it this far into the workbook—not you folks who started here to see how the story ended!—you are doing very well. I am really proud of you that you have followed along this painful, challenging, but, eventually, so rewarding path of healing for yourself, your partner, and your relationship.

You've been to the depths and back, experienced the unimaginable, and held yourself in the spaces of pain and longing with your partner who is also willing and able to lay themselves open and vulnerable with you, to help your relationship grow strong, close, loving, and safe.

The hope is that having made it to this point in the process, when the two of you find yourselves in conflict, you will be able to draw upon your mentalizing and emotion regulation skills to navigate conflicts with clarity, tolerable and manageable emotions, and the ability to see one another's perspectives. With these, you may find your way to a co-created solution that you both can feel good about and follow through with. Having worked hard to push through the stuck spots, which are often forces outside of our awareness that block the smooth path forward, you have become more able to engage in building earned security through your practice of Secure Base Behaviours. Go forth and feel confident in your capacity to help each other to regulate your emotional states, even when the going gets tough. Keep practising and trying, pushing through the pull of the path, and continue your movement from insecurity to earned security.

The overall goal of Stage Four is to help you more easily access these self-capacities and new ways of experiencing and being with one another when faced with stress, especially when your attachment systems are activated due to normal couple conflict. I don't expect that life will become easy just because you have completed this workbook. Rather, I hope that you will be able to support and soothe one another when the going gets rough, to turn towards each other instead of away, when the challenges of life press heavily down upon you. Over time, I hope that you will be able to draw upon your newly developed self-capacities as simply a part of you, automatic responses, and to trust your new earned secure attachment as something that you can rely upon and always come back to.

Over time, as you continue to practise the new skills and capacities, ways of being and reflecting, you will turn towards each other in your distress, to comfort one another, and

DOI: 10.4324/9781003330950-26

tolerate your differences and differing needs without losing mentalizing and emotion regulation capacities. With these in place, you will become more able to compromise and solve problems together without getting pulled into your negative cycles or DTRs. And my hope for you is that you finally experience what it is like to live in the present, deal with the usual ups and downs, stresses and strains of life, and not be pulled back by traumas that are being repeated within your relationship. Go slowly, go back to sections where you need more practice and, gradually, you'll automatically be pulling yourself out of conflicts and applying your new skills and abilities as though they were second nature.

CHECKLIST FOR PULLING IT ALL TOGETHER

When you find yourself in a conflict that threatens to escalate into pulling you into your negative cycle and throw you into your DTR, take a breath and answer the following questions with your partner:

What am I feeling in my body? Am I breathing? Am I feeling oriented to what is happening right here, right now, between us?

_____

_____

_____

_____

On a scale of 1–10, how regulated am I? Can I think, breathe, speak, feel my body, comfortably?

_____

_____

_____

_____

On a scale of 1–10, how co-regulated are we? Are we able to gaze at one another, share our thoughts and feelings, breathe in synchronicity, and turn to one another in this distress?

_____

_____

_____

_____

On a scale of 1–10, how regulated am I in my own mentalizing? Am I able to be curious, am I falling into making assumptions, am I no longer hearing what my partner is saying and, instead, filling in my own narrative?

_____

_____

_____

_____

On a scale of 1–10, how regulated are we as a couple in our shared mentalizing? Are we both able to be curious, are we making assumptions about each other, are we hearing each other?

_____

_____

_____

_____

Are we falling into our negative cycle? If so, am I able to hold onto and regulate my pursuit/withdrawal? Is my partner able to hold onto and regulate their pursuit/withdrawal? Are we able to talk about our cycle and stop it before it takes off and escalates?

_____

_____

_____

_____

Are we falling into our DTR? If so, am I able to reflect and regulate my own absorption into the past and keep it separate from this interaction? Is my partner able to reflect and regulate their absorption into the past and keep it separate from this interaction? Are we able to talk about what traumatic DTR material is getting activated and stop it before it takes off and escalates?

_____

_____

_____

_____

What are five things that we can both agree on to try if we are struggling to pull ourselves out of absorbing states of distress?

_____

_____

_____

_____

What is one thing that is guaranteed to make us laugh even if we are in the hole of messiness? Do either of us get to pull that one out of our back pocket?

_____

_____

_____

_____

What is one thing that we can agree upon will always be a safe form of emotional contact if we are getting stuck in a dysregulated, non-mentalizing conflict?

_____

_____

_____

_____

What is one thing that we can agree upon will always be a safe form of physical contact if we are getting stuck in a dysregulated, non-mentalizing conflict? Do you require consent for this kind of contact? If there is nothing that you can yet agree upon, keep coming back to the question until such time as you feel able to identify something.

_____

_____

_____

_____

What is one very special thing about each other that you always want to remember when you are struggling in moments of conflict and distress?

_____

_____

_____

_____

If either or both of you are creatives, you might take your answer to that last question and immortalize it in some form of visual representation that you can put on the wall and silently point to, if necessary, when you are having a hard time. When we are feeling all the hard feelings, we need to be reminded of who we are to one another. One of the greatest gifts for me, as a person with a lot of avoidance and not a lot of capacity to hold attachment, is that my partner is a musician and has recorded some of her own music. I can always find her in there, even if I can't find her across the living room. Hold tight to the ways in which your partner touches your deep loving self, even when they may be hard to find.

I wish I could give you some magic words and send you off into the world knowing that all things are now well, and you will no longer struggle as a human in the world or a partner in a relationship. I wish I could take away the pain, trauma, and vulnerability that you carry. While I cannot give you those things, I have given you what I have to give: my story, what I have learned from the hours, days, months and years of being with our fellow travellers on this journey to healing. I send you courage for this journey. Keep going, stop for rests, and always bring snacks. I'm proud of you for making it this far. I hope for you rest, gentleness, a love no longer tainted by those who have hurt you, and quiet in your self, free from the intrusions of the past and filled with the river of life that calls you and your partner to closeness, security, safety, and laughter that spills out to all of the spaces and places you inhabit.

Index

Accepting and Acknowledging (exercise) 217–19

Adopting a Mentalizing Stance (exercise) 96–8

Adopting a Mentalizing Stance in a Low Stakes Role Play (journal reflection) 98–9

anger: as primary or secondary emotion 26–7; safe expression 5

anxious attachment 41–2

approach-avoid tango 42

asexuality 184

Attachment and Trauma (journal reflection) 43–7

attachment styles 42–3; and couple dynamics 112

avoidance 144, 231

avoidant attachment 41–2

basic emotions *see* primary and secondary emotions

Behaviour, Affect, Sensation, and Knowledge (BASK) 163–4

BIPOC survivors: and shame 31; and trauma 13

bodies: and co-regulation 89, 155; and trauma 57, 64; as battlegrounds 53, 162, 180–1; reliving trauma 84, 161

body dysmorphia 142

body memories *see* flashbacks

Bondage Domination Sado-Masochism (BDSM) 185

caregivers: and emotion regulation 21, 63, 80, 105; unsupportive 94, 142, 219

Catching and Changing (exercise) 219–20

childhood trauma: and sexuality 176–7; impact on adults 54; impact on attachment 41; sharing 144

co-regulation: and identifying emotions 71; impact of trauma 63

Co-regulation (journal reflection) 80–1

conflict: and mentalizing 100, 227; and secure base behaviours 124; and sexuality 185; *see also* Dyadic Traumatic Reenactment (DTR)

consent: and communication 184–5; and sexual secrets 195; and touch 64

Consistency and Change (journal reflection) 118

Consistency of Attachment (journal reflection) 120–1

couple therapy: and mentalizing 35; and negative cycles 48; *see also* Developmental Couple Therapy for Complex Trauma (DCTCT)

Developmental Couple Therapy for Complex Trauma (DCTCT) 2; background and purpose 6–7; manual 9, 26, 34, 214, 227; role of therapist 107, 146, 156, 160, 161–2, 173, 200, 213–14, 219; stages 3–4

disclosure: and trauma recovery 141; setting the stage 145; sexual secrets 201; sharing 154–6

dissociation 56, 86–7, 157, 196, 201

DTR Worksheet (exercise) 222–3

Dyadic Emotional Coping, Deeper Exploration (exercise) 82–6

Dyadic Emotional Coping, Initial Exploration (exercise) 81–2

dyadic regulation 88–90

Dyadic Traumatic Reenactment (DTR) 49; and couple therapy 213; and negative cycles 48–9; catching and changing 219–20; challenges and strategies 209

Dyadic Traumatic Reenactment (journal reflection) 210–12

Earned Security 42–3, 112–15, 119, 134, 140, 173, 176, 201, 209, 219, 227
emotion regulation 22; and self-regulation 63, 71; and co-regulation 83; and consolidation 227; and developmental trauma 21; and mentalizing 106–7; and trauma 18; strategies 63–7
Emotion Regulation, Trauma, and Couples (journal reflection) 24–5
emotional support: and sharing 139; and triggers 173; during disclosure 155
emotionally focused therapy (EFT) 2
Emotions and Childhood Trauma (handout), 21–2
empathy 18; see also mentalizing
exercises, Stage One: Identify the Negative Cycle 50
exercises, Stage Three: Accepting and Acknowledging 217–19; Catching and Changing 219–20; DTR Worksheet 222–3; Finding Your Way to Your Own Sexual Body 186–9; Making a List Together 171–2; Navigating Triggers 192–5; Noticing and Naming 215–17; Secure Base Behaviour 128–40
exercises, Stage Two: Adopting a Mentalizing Stance 96–8; Dyadic Emotional Coping, Deeper Exploration 82–6; Dyadic Emotional Coping, Initial Exploration 81–2; Exploring Learned Emotional Relationships 77–8; Feelings Identification Exercises 71–4; Mentalizing Skill Building 100–4; Name That Feeling! 70–6; Regulation and Rhythm: Dyadic 88–90; Regulation and Rhythm: Individual 86–7; Square Breathing 65–7
Exploring Learned Emotional Relationships (exercise) 77–8
exposure (therapy technique) 163

Family, Culture, and Sex (journal reflection) 177–80
Feelings Chart 69–70
Feelings Identification Exercises (exercises) 71–4
feelings see primary and secondary emotions
Finding Your Sexuality (journal reflection) 190–1
flashbacks 145, 164, 173
For Partners (journal reflection) 169–70

gaslighting (form of manipulation) 105–7
gender dysphoria 142

gender transition: and sexual healing 188; and co-regulation 207; and puberty 205; and trauma 4, 53, 206

handouts, Stage One: Emotions and Childhood Trauma 21–2; How Trauma Impacts Individuals 12; Impact of Trauma on Couples 17–18; Mentalizing 34–6; Negative Cycles and Dyadic Traumatic Reenactment 48–9; Sex and Sexuality After Trauma 54–5; Shame 30–1; Trauma and Attachment 40–1
handouts, Stage Two: Mentalizing Skill Building Cheat Sheet 104
Healing Broken Bonds: addressing individual trauma 162; how to navigate 6–7; purpose and format 2; self-study 7
How are We Changing? (journal reflection) 173–5
How Do I Understand Mentalizing? (journal reflection) 92–4
How Trauma Impacts Individuals (handout) 12

"I" language 140
Identify the Negative Cycle (exercise) 50
identities: cultural 177; embodied 85
Imagining the Inside From the Outside (journal reflection) 95–6
Impact of Trauma on Couple Relationships (journal reflection) 18–20
Impact of Trauma on Couples (handout) 17–18
Impacts of Trauma (journal reflections) 14–16
insecure attachment 40
Internal Working Model (IWM) 42–3, 113, 119, 121–2, 133–4, 144, 209
intimacy 144, 163

Johnson, Dr. Sue 2
journal reflections, Stage One: Attachment and Trauma 43–7; Emotion Regulation, Trauma, and Couples 24–5; Impact of Trauma on Couple Relationships 18–20; Impacts of Trauma 14–16; Mentalizing 38–9; Negative Cycle and DTR 51–2; Primary and Secondary Emotions 28; Shame and Your Relationship 32–3; Trauma, Sex, and Sexuality 57–9
journal reflections, Stage Three: Consistency and Change 118; Consistency of Attachment 120–1; Dyadic Traumatic Reenactment

210–12; Family, Culture, and Sex
177–80; Finding Your Sexuality 190–1; For
Partners 169–70; How are We Changing?
173–5; Other Kinds of Secrets 158–9; Our
Relationship with Our Body 181–4; Review
111–12; Secure Base Behaviours Chart
125–8; Sexual Secrets 197–200; Sharing
Sexual Secrets 202–3; Traumatic Memories
and Your Relationship 165–7; Your
Attachment Style 115–17
journal reflections, Stage Two: Adopting a
Mentalizing Stance in a Low Stakes Role
Play 98–9; Co-Regulation 80–1; How Do I
Understand Mentalizing? 92–4; Imagining
the Inside From the Outside 95–6; Learned
Emotional Relationships 78–9; Name That
Feeling! 76–7; Regulation and Rhythm:
Dyadic 90; Regulation and Rhythm:
Individual 87–8; Square Breathing 67–8

Learned Emotional Relationships (journal
reflection) 78–9
LGBTQ survivors: sexuality and childhood
abuse 142; and shame 31; and trauma 13

Making a List Together (exercise) 171–2
mentalizing 34; and consolidation 227; and
partner abuse 105–7; characteristics 36;
examples 37; in couples 94; in relationships
207; struggles 37–8
Mentalizing (handout) 34–6
Mentalizing (journal reflection) 38–9
Mentalizing Skill Building (exercise) 100–4
Mentalizing Skill Building Cheat Sheet
(handout) 104
Model Scenes (impactful memories) 134, 145

Name That Feeling! (exercise) 70–6
Name That Feeling! (journal reflection) 76–7
Negative Cycle and DTR (journal reflection)
51–2
Negative Cycles and Dyadic Traumatic
Reenactment (handout) 48–9
negative interaction cycles see Dyadic
Traumatic Reenactment (DTR)
non-binary survivors 142
non-monogamy 205
Noticing and Naming (exercise) 215–17

Other Kinds of Secrets (journal reflection)
158–9
Our Relationship With Our Body (journal
reflection) 181–4

parallel play 156
polyamory 205
preoccupied attachment 41–2
primary and secondary emotions 26; chart 27;
identifying 69–70
Primary and Secondary Emotions (journal
reflection) 28

queer survivors 142

Regulation and Rhythm: Dyadic (exercise) 88–90
Regulation and Rhythm: Dyadic (journal
reflection) 90
Regulation and Rhythm: Individual (exercise)
86–7
Regulation and Rhythm: Individual (journal
reflection) 87–8
Review (journal reflection) 111–12
role play: and sexuality 176, 204; mentalizing
exercise 96–8

secrets: in partner relationships 157–8; see also
sexual secrets
secure attachment 40
Secure Base Behaviour (exercise) 128–40
Secure Base Behaviour Exercise Step One:
Identifying the Weak Link in the Sequence
(handout) 129–33
Secure Base Behaviour Exercise Step Two:
Identifying the Link to Early Development
(Handout) 134–9
Secure Base Behaviour Exercise Step Three:
Strategies for Change 139–40
Secure Base Behaviours 121–40; and
attachment 121; and consolidation 227;
and sharing 154
Secure Base Behaviours Chart (journal
reflection) 125–8
self-help books 1
self-regulation: and identifying emotions 71;
impact of trauma 63
sex: compatibility 176; self-exploration 187
Sex and Sexuality after Trauma (handout) 54–5
sexual secrets: and consent 195–6; disclosing
201; healing 204
Sexual Secrets (journal reflection) 197–200
sexuality: and conflict 176; and language
177; and secrets 195–6; and trauma 18, 53,
109, 142, 180; and triggers 192; reducing
bifurcation 204–5
shame: and disclosure 141; and Dyadic
Traumatic Reenactment (DTR) 213; and
relationships 31, 83; and secrets 158; and

sexuality 201, 205; as primary or secondary emotion 29–30; overcoming 110
Shame (handout) 30–1
Shame and Your Relationship (journal reflection) 32–3
sharing: and boundaries 154; and triggers 168
Sharing Sexual Secrets (journal reflection) 202–3
Square Breathing (exercise) 65–7
Square Breathing (journal reflection) 67–8

Telling the Story (exercise) 145–55
trans and non-binary survivors 142
trauma: and identity 13; impact on mentalizing 35; impact on relationships 55; unlinked from memory 163

Trauma and Attachment (handout) 40–1
trauma processing 162
Trauma, Sex, and Sexuality (journal reflection) 57–9
Traumatic Memories and Your Relationship (journal reflection) 165–7
triggers: and couple dynamics 213; avoidable and unavoidable 195; navigating 170–1, 192; sharing 168

violence: and oppression 56; interpersonal 53, 162, 206

Your Attachment Style (journal reflection) 115–17

For Product Safety Concerns and Information please contact our EU
representative GPSR@taylorandfrancis.com
Taylor & Francis Verlag GmbH, Kaufingerstraße 24, 80331 München, Germany

www.ingramcontent.com/pod-product-compliance
Lightning Source LLC
Chambersburg PA
CBHW080132270326
41926CB00021B/4444

9 781032 362465